BUILD
UNIVERSES

Brian Winder

A Search for a Son

europe books

© 2021 **Europe Books** | London
www.europebooks.co.uk – info@europebooks.co.uk

ISBN 979-12-201-0674-0
First edition: July 2021

Distribution for the United Kingdom: **Vine House Distribution ltd**

Printed for Italy by Rotomail Italia
Finito di stampare nel mese di luglio 2021
presso Rotomail Italia S.p.A. - Vignate (MI)

A Search for a Son

"Let not young souls be smothered out before
They do quaint deeds and fully flaunt their pride.
It is the world's one crime its babes grow dull..."

—Vachel Lindsay

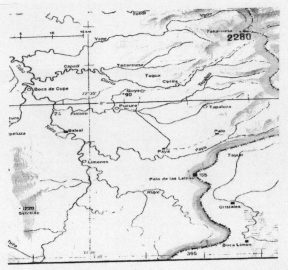

Lost in the jungle

In March Paul Winder, 29, and Tom Hart Dyke, 24, disappeared in the treacherous jungle between Panama and Colombia. As Tom's mother, Sarah, arrives in Panama, Paul's father, Brian Winder, describes his search for the boys

Who knows what makes one person avoid danger and another embrace it? Maybe it is because he was a silly youngster that Paul started enjoying risky adventures as he grew older. The first time he went on a long trip, about six years ago, he was out off by revolutionaries in the Sahara desert for two months. Of course we were desperately worried and nearly flew out, but the incident ended happily. Perhaps that is why we were slower to react this time.

Last October Paul arranged sabbatical leave from Salomon Brothers, the bank where he works in the City, for what was to be, he promised us, his last big trip. He is 29 now and after this we expected him to settle down. He moved back home for a few months to save for his trip and told us that he had always been fascinated by the Darien Gap, the passage from North to South America. To Paul, this was true exploration.

We accepted this decision, as we had

year. However, even with his house on stilts he sleeps with a metal sheet under him at night in case anyone sticks a machete through the floorboards to kill him. He told us how one night he was walking home after buying a chicken when someone from a passing truck hit him on the head with a beer bottle. When he woke up, he had a gash in his head, no chicken, no shirt and no trousers, and two of his gold teeth — a local status symbol — had been chipped out.

The Darien is even more of a no-go area. The Panama-Colombia border runs along the watershed with mountains about the height of the Pennines. In the middle is the Darien Gap, an area of jungle so dangerous that no-one dares to live there. It is notoriously overrun by left-wing guerrillas, right-wing paramilitaries and freelance brigands who kill even for the coins in your pocket. The occasional drug-runner passes through but most are too frightened to use this route. The Panamanian and Colombian armies are themselves afraid to enter the area. It is marked on the map as the Palo

TOP: MAP OF DARIAN IN PANAMA
BOTTOM: PUBLICITY IN JULY by BRIAN WINDER

Freed jungle Britons return to captors and ask for map

SAFE: Tom Hart Dyke, the Indiana Jones of British botany

SAFE: Paul Winder who believed Tom he kept was suicide

TOP BEFORE CHRISTMAS: THE LAST DANGEROUS
STEP BEFORE ESCAPE
BOTTOM: CELEBATING AT LULLIGSTONE CASTLE IN THE SNOW
OF WINTER: LEFT TO RIGHT: TOM, JAMES SPRING, PAUL

TOM HART DYKE & PAUL WINDER

The CLOUD GARDEN

A TRUE STORY OF ADVENTURE, SURVIVAL AND EXTREME HORTICULTURE

Thursday, April 24, 2003   Page X

Conman's lies over missing Lucie cost father £15,000

Michael Hills: Deception

By Ron Newling

A GHOULISH conman who exploited a terrified father's desperation to find his missing daughter is today facing jail.

Michael Hills, 59, tricked £15,500 out of the father of murdered air hostess Lucie Blackman by claiming he had underworld contacts who could find her.

She had disappeared in Japan in July 2000.

He also claimed he could produce a lock of the 21-year-old's hair to prove she was alive.

Tim Blackman, who believed Hills's lies, handed over the cash.

He even flew to Japan after Hills claimed Lucie would be released at a particular date and time.

But yesterday Hills pleaded guilty to two counts of obtaining property by deception.

Mr Blackman, 48, said: 'Part of me still wonders if he could have made a difference but the overwhelming feeling I have is of disgust and abomination.

'He infiltrated my life with completely false promises and lies – it

is just despicable really. I hope that they will come down as far as they can on him.'

Chelmsford Crown Court yesterday heard that Hills attempted a similar scam on Brian Winder, the father of Paul Winder, who went missing in South America but was eventually released.

Judge Rodger Hayward Smith, QC, adjourned the case for sentence, but said the chances of Hills escaping jail were 'remote'.

Hills is thought to have contacted the Winder and Blackman families after reading about their plight in a newspaper article.

Mr Blackman, a property developer, first met the conman in Belgium after he contacted the family through the British Embassy in Tokyo.

During the meeting Hills said he had information that could help in tracing Lucie, of Sevenoaks, Kent, and in later e-mails to Mr Black-

man he made even more wild promises.

Investigating officer DC Brendan Cox said: 'The deception became graver because it became more and more over time a promise that he would find her.'

Mr Blackman ended up handing over £15,500 to Hills.

His daughter's remains were eventually found in a cave near Tokyo in February 2001. A Japanese man is due to stand trial for her murder this summer.

Hills lies came to light after he tried a smaller scam on Brian Winder, whose son was missing by South American guerrillas in March 2000.

Mr Winder ended up handing over £6,000 before he became suspicious and alerted the police.

He also contacted the Blackmans as he realised that both the families' stories had featured in a newspaper article that he thought

Hills must have read. Mr Winder, 67, of Great Baddow, Essex, said Hills went to great lengths to convince his victims of his power.

But rather than anger Mr Winder said he felt pity for Hills.

He said: 'It could make Lord Of The Rings, then he is a a Gollum-type character, a creature of the underworld for whom I feel pity, although at the time he caused us a lot of distress.'

Arriving yesterday at the B&B

where he lives, in Lower Marsh, Waterloo, South London, Hills claimed he had been working at the residences for Japanese Mafia.

He said all the money was handed over to his underworld contacts.

Asked what he would say to Mr Blackman now, he replied: 'Just sorry. What can I say to Blackman? Can I get his daughter back? No.'

Lucie: A Japanese man is to stand trial for her murder

TOP THE CLOUD GARDEN: PAUL & TOM'S STORY
BOTTOM THE COURT CSE FOR DECEIT

A dream that saved my life

When Tom Hart Dyke was kidnapped by Colombian guerrillas, he kept his sanity by planning an elaborate 'garden of the world'. Four years on, he has started to build it. .

TOP AFTERMATH: TOM'S WOLD GARDEN
BOTTOM: PAUL'S MOUNTAINEERING

Index

1
INTRODUCTION: THE VICISSITUDES OF LIFE

As I lay on my hospital bed after a prostate cancer operation in January 2000, I wondered if my cancer would really be cured or would I die at a relatively early age.

Six months later, all was changed.

I could not give two hoots whether I lived or died.

All that concerned me was whether my son, Paul, was dead in the jungles of Central America.

I could think of nothing else.

Summer, winter, I hardly noticed the seasons.

The family had spent most of their summer holiday when the kids were young camping in France and exploring the mountains.

When in their teens the kids no longer fancied such, I had gone with Paul, the eldest, to the high Alps once on a Glacier course around Chamonix, once just by ourselves in the high Alps and once ascending Mount Blanc. On that last, I am afraid that my lack of fitness and our joint not acclimatising ourselves properly to the height caused us to give up before the final shoulder of the mountain and not achieving our goal.

So, I had a certain affinity with Paul.

Paul had, of course, long since grown into his independence and had lived away from home for some years and had slipped from 28 to 29 years old during this search.

The rest of this narrative will show that, for the greater

part, we endured our search for Paul with a Northern European stiff upper lip, but there was, of course, turmoil within. But because of the uncertainty of the outcome, our mood was more frustration than tearfulness.

And when the situation became public because of our appearance on TV, there was the embarrassed silence of friends not asking how things were going because they assumed the news was still bad and any question might make us emotional.

2
FLOUNDERING IN A FOG

What do you do when a son or a daughter goes missing?

A family member is said to go missing every 10 minutes in the UK. The journalists seem to ignore 99.9% of the instances and pick up the stories of one or two at random – when news is short. They make a great fuss about that one, even if he is only missing for a few days. But should you make a fuss? Should you cause public money to be wasted on a private family affair?

We felt that when our eldest son, Paul, went missing in Panama, we should not make a fuss, so we did not make any enquiries almost for the first 3 months after we got the last card or email from him. Besides, Paul had disappeared in the south of Panama, which is roughly 6000 miles away. Who does a parent enquire of 6000 miles away in a Spanish speaking country?

But waiting has been eliminated from our DNA nowadays. A hundred years ago, a member of the family would go off to another continent, and the people at home often didn't expect a letter from them ever again – and certainly not a visit home. With increased literacy and the phone and moderately cheap airfares, we nowadays expect continued contact. But the huge step forward came at the end of the 20th century with the instant access of the internet and the banks of information available. We have come to expect to be able to find out anything on anything without delay.

When our son, Paul, went missing in March 2000, we didn't react quickly. Young men don't want parents fussing over them. So we took our time. The last card we got from him was dated March 7th 2000, and it was from the small town of Yaviza in southern Panama. It announced that he was "going to do some serious trekking": but it not specifically mention where he was going or if he had a companion or intended to have a guide.

But one thing that complicated it was that Paul had sent us an email while in Panama City saying that he had met a chap with a boat sailing to Australia from Equador in early April and he was looking for crew, and Paul might take that opportunity to experience crossing the Pacific in a small yacht.

So, nothing seemed certain.

We found Yaviza on the map. We worried a little, but not too much. We were both busy, Anne in teaching, myself in a consultancy. Paul had been out of contact in the Sahara for 2 months in a previous adventure, so we were a little used to it.

The rest of March passed. April came and went. No card, no contact. In May we contacted the Foreign Office and the Panamanian and Colombian embassies in London. The delays in getting a reply varied between a few weeks in the case of the first two and a few months with the Colombian Embassy, all of them basically saying that they knew nothing. But then people were always disappearing in Colombia. So it seemed that those official channels were useless.

I decided to keep a diary – for the first time in my adult

life. How long will it take to know what has happened – a week, a month, a year or never – to know if he is alive or dead? There is a great thirst to know.

A Brief Backtrack

Paul had worked long hours with Saloman Brothers in wholesale banking in London for the last 2 years or so, and had lived away from home for the last 5 years. He obviously was bored by lunchtime drinks in London pubs, where people just talked about cars and other irrelevant things.

What interested him was going on trips. Home was a place where he could stay for a while cheaply before or after a trip.

Later he travelled around Europe without pre-booking accommodation and on one occasion sussed out where the family were camping in an obscure location in the backwoods of Germany. He hitch-hiked his way there in a day. That was before the days of satnavs and I-phones.

Later his trips abroad were inclined to last for many months, and were funded by his work. His first long trip had been over the Sahara Desert and down Western Africa to Zaire, then thumbing lifts over the almost impassable roads of Zaire to the East Coast of Africa. His second trip was to Australasia, Indonesia etc. He always concentrated on going off the beaten track.

Now he announced that he was taking time off to do another trip – this time to the Americas, and especially Spanish America – Mexico and southwards – the highlight being the difficult transition from North to South America.

He had said that this would probably be his last trip. Would it be his last trip in a different sense from what he meant?

I accepted Paul's new trip as a father would normally accept it – with interest and amusement: I had travelled in the '60s in the long teacher's holidays behind the Iron Curtain and in North Africa.

Also I had worked for 11 years in Africa, speaking a local language – knowing more closely than a tourist ever would a society other than my own.

If I hadn't known the fact that most of what one eventually finds out from travel is about oneself, I might have envied Paul.

Paul was tolerant enough of us, and accepted Anne's offer to take him to the airport. I didn't want to lay it on thick, so I didn't go. Off he went, but Anne kept her worries and 'all these things in her heart' – the heart always a certain amount in the mouth. That was in October 1999.

An e-mail or a card every 4 to 6 weeks was what we expected. Otherwise we got on with our busy lives.

We got a few e-mails from Paul in the intervening months. Here's one in early January.

"A bit late but I hope you all had a Merry Christmas, and will have a happy New Year. I'm in Guatemala celebrating, though there was an election on Boxing Day, so Christmas Day was dry.
Traveller's tales of bandits. Two of us thought we didn't need a guide for the Volcano San Pedro, we'd just go up.

We got lost, took the wrong path, struggled through thick jungle, almost trod on a snake, then gave up a few hundred feet from the top.

On the day after, another group of travellers had got to the top, where bandits relieved them of everything: they had to walk down naked into the village: hilarious! We found out when we got down that we had taken the correct path after all... but it's lucky we gave up!

I've also been ruining myself in Mexico Teotihuacan, Palenque, Calakmul, plus Tikal, and then relaxing in Belize.

Belize is a great crazy place to have a drink with the locals, to canoe along the rivers in the jungle: lots of crocs and a tropical paradise on the Cayes.

I was able to swim with nurse sharks, cuddle them and tickle their tummies...

Though not all is heaven here: I missed a shoot-out at the Oceanside bar by a week: two drunken policemen got a little carried away, and the day before I left a Rastafarian hung himself just off the main street..."

But that was an unusually informative e-mail. Most e-mails were asking me of what was left on his Barclaycard.

Since my cancer operation in January 2000, I had been concentrating on learning to walk again, and doing as much of my work and other activities as I could.

Anne had her teaching absorbing her waking moments, as most teachers do.

End of Back-track and to May 2000 again

By May I was trying to search the internet in case there might be any clues. Our middle son, Bill, did some research and found Paul had two email addresses, with two different providers. In mid-May Bill broke into one of them, but it obviously wasn't used much. There were only two correspondents on it, a Mike Pearson and a Murray Vissor. Bill e-mailed them.

Mike Pearson described his meeting Paul in Panama City and Paul saying that he intended to go through the Darien Gap with a person named Tom. Mike went on: "I have heard a lot of unpleasant stuff about the Darien, and have not heard from Paul since. Although I have written to him several times, hoping to elicit a reply, it's now been well over 2 months since I got a reply. I have also asked other travellers going the same way in the hope that someone has seen him.

I know that he is very capable and experienced, but must admit to being worried. The Darien can be an extremely dangerous place, and few travellers chance it these days.

I had thought that he may have tried the Darien, found that he couldn't safely make it through and flown home. However, your e-mail shows that this is not the case, and I am now more worried than ever. I believe that it should have taken him no more than 2 weeks to cross from Panama to Columbia, from where he could easily send e-mails."

So, this Mike was really worried, and it made us worried.

We also got another e-mail from Mike Pearson – but with rather impractical suggestions: "Search for this Tom by going through all Panamanian immigration records for male UK citizens starting with the letter T, and entering Panama by land from Costa Rica 2 to 4 weeks after Paul. You might also try e-mailing Patricia Upton."

That name would occur again.

Mike Pearson also mentioned a Frank from Switzerland,

who had met Paul in Nicaragua and had said that he intended to go down to Colombia: just a possibility.

The many suggestions were bewildering and difficult for me to chase up with my limited Spanish.

Meanwhile, we searched around for books and maps: one book told about three American missionaries who were kidnapped in the Darien in 1994. A ransom of $3,000,000 was asked for them. It was not paid, and they had never been heard of since, so presumably, they were killed.

But Mike Pearson did provide us with a slight advance in our knowledge: that Paul had gone with a companion, a fellow called Tom.

It only made us desirous to find out more.

Murray Vissor replied with just a little more information. Paul had said to him that he wanted to go "up the middle" of the Darien Gap, not along either East or West coast which were far safer. As for the possibility of a travelling companion named Tom, Murray said that the only Tom he knew that Paul could have met was a lawyer from San Francisco, who was very limited in the time he had available to travel. But we could find no such Tom on Paul's first email site. So, a dead-end there.

And then Murray tried to put me off going to the Darien to try to follow Paul's trail: "There are lots of diseases there: cholera, rabies, malaria...

Panamanian bandits hide out there like American bandits in the Wild West 100 years ago... and the rainy season has started, making it impossible... and I just don't know what you could achieve by going there yourself: you'll be just imitating Paul who ignored all the advice given him..."

All rather encouraging stuff!

May 18th was Paul's birthday. Anne sent an e-mail: "Happy birthday. We haven't heard from you for a long time and are very concerned. We heard that you were going through the Darien Gap. Please contact us. Love. Mum".

We both wondered if it would ever reach him. At work I phoned our son Bill and said, "I think there will be some tears at home tonight."

From that point on, I was preparing to go to Panama and try to follow Paul's likely route. I got books and tapes for Spanish out of the library, but it was not easy to revive my simple Spanish of 35 years previously. The plan for my visit to Panama would be to follow Paul's probable trail through the "middle" of the Darien Gap from Yaviza. I booked a flight for late May to Panama.

The Darien Gap is on the border between Panama and Colombia. There is no road from North to South America. The Pan-American Highway stops well before the border. All travel is by river in that area.

There had been a guerrilla war going on for many years in Colombia, and the guerrillas occupied the dense jungle on the border. The area is so dangerous that there is no police or army presence even long before the border, and it was a lawless country. There is a National Park on the Colombian side of the Darien Gap, but it had been closed and the Ranger Stations in it had been deserted since about 1995 because of the danger – both from the FARC guerillas and from the right-wing paramilitaries. The paramilitaries were largely the Colombian army with their uniforms off.

We decided to get the British Embassy in Panama to make enquiries of the Panama police. But the police only came back asking for Paul's passport number and the exact date and point of his entering the country and a list of all countries that Paul had visited before coming to Panama, and his teeth x rays. We gave them what they wanted, but we thought it seemed like the police in Zambia where we lived for 8 years: they were only stalling.

Bill, Paul's brother, suggested taking an armed guard. I mentioned this to the British Embassy, who vehemently opposed it. They were very much against going into the Darien area at all. We asked if they could find a guide for us, but again they seemed to have no contacts. It took us a little time to realise that the British embassy was there to help make trade and commercial contacts, not to waste their time on silly tourists.

I still told the Embassy that I intended to go to the Darien in the immediate future and that I was fully aware of the dangers of the area and of the problems of the rainy season. I asked them how I would arrange internal flights from Panama City to El Real, and possibly get a National Park pass.

The embassy did indeed make enquires of the police in Yaviza and Boca de Cupe about Paul, but it came back that the police there – as always – knew nothing. The policy seemed to be out to hide everything. They did not want it to gain publicity and thus to discourage tourists to Panama – a valid enough point of view.

At this stage we were naïve enough to search the Internet for travel agents who organised tours to the Darien. Adverts still hung on the Internet from years before for such tours, but they had all given up going there.

My nephew, Kieran, found a detective agency, who advertise finding missing people, and faxed me the questionnaire they issue when they take on a new client.

"What are the telephone numbers of close personal friends of theirs?

What nicknames might they use for each other?

What were their hobbies?

Were they planning to phone home?

What kind of hotels do they stay in?"

Those questions may be relevant to a teenager who runs away in the UK… but I am certain that the agency has no experience of such places as the Darien rain-forest; nor would they be willing to go there. Or if they went there bristling with arms, they would be soon stopped by the police, or worst still provoke a shoot-out with the guerrillas.

We could imagine such a detective slinking along to some Bogota disco and listening out for their using these nicknames to each other – not searching for them in the jungle, where there are no hotels or discos, and hobbies are irrelevant.

So, the agency didn't look impressive. It started off with the slogan, "Everyone can be found." I thought that motto meant, "We want your money." So, I did not take it further.

By now the sum of our knowledge was that Paul had planned to take the route through the centre of the Darien Gap, and that he talked of a companion whose name was Tom.

But whether he had finally taken that route or who that companion called Tom was, or whether he had hired a guide or not, we did not know. We were at a loss as to what to do next. All avenues of research seemed to be closed, and I knew I had to do something on the spot, so I continued to plan to visit Panama.

What do you do when all roads to information seemed blocked?

Friends rallied around, but we were no further forward.

My son, Bill, somehow made contact with the BBC correspondent in Colombia, Jerry McDermott, who sent me a helpful and sympathetic memo with interesting information: "I can imagine what you are going through, and if I can be of any assistance, please do not hesitate to ask.

I have been in Latin America for two years and know the Darien and northern Colombia very well.

As I am sure you are already aware, the Darien is an area in which FARC guerrillas and AUC paramilitaries have been very active. It is an area which the security forces of both sides, Panama and Colombia, fear to go. It is a lawless area.

If Paul has fallen into FARC hands, they will be making enquiries as to who he is and what he is worth. You will already be aware that Colombia is the kidnap capital of the world. Matters do move slowly with them, especially since the front that would have got him would be one of the usual "kidnapping" fronts and so it may take a great deal of time for them to do their research and issue a ransom demand. If the FARC have him, then he is relatively safe. They do not kill Brits without reason, and he will be seen by them as simply an item of business, as that is what kidnapping is to them.

If the paramilitaries got him, then they would have interrogated him and let him go.

What worries me is smugglers, common criminals, nature or an accident.

On the Colombian side it might be worth speaking directly to the government department which deals with kidnapping, called the Presidential Programme for the Defence of Personal Liberty: although, if they had heard anything of Paul, they would have already contacted the British Embassy. But it might serve as a kick in the arse for them to go and make some enquiries.

Speak to the British Embassy in Panama and ask them to shake the tree a little, for the DAS (secret police) to make some enquiries and the national police. They will probably tell you that there is no evidence that Paul ever came to Colombia so it is not their problem.

On the Panamanian side there are said to be police units that patrol the Darien. I went down to Puerto Obaldia in January and went to speak to them. If anybody has an idea, it will be them. They will be able to tell you about what has been going on there, and they have links with the Colombian police across the border.

I could try contacting the FARC and ask them if they had Paul... but little more apart from banging on doors.

I am sorry I have not been of more help. I will keep Paul in my mind and see if I can think of something else.

I have married a Colombian and I worry every day about her safety.

Please keep in touch if you feel I can help, and I will keep my ear to the ground..."

Another relative, Stephen, my nephew in Ireland, has set up an internet site called FINDPAUL, and has recorded the basic facts of the case there. Also by searching the internet under "Darien" he found an Alexandro Jaimes who seems to live in New York but comes from Colombia. He had been a volunteer a few years ago in the Katios National Park, which is what "the central route" of the Darien goes straight through once it enters Colombia.

He recommended contacting the Ministry of the Environment in Colombia, since they are in charge of the parks. He offered various phone numbers. But the phone is difficult for me with my almost forgotten Spanish, and the 6-hour time-lag makes it challenging to get a hold of people in the working day who are better at Spanish. So I've asked Alexandro to do some contacting for me (perhaps forgetting that he was in New York). He is going to ask the Park authorities if Paul Winder is recorded as being present in the Katios National Park.

But these few email contacts were not solving the problem: where did Paul finally go to and with whom.

I then realised that I simply had not enough information gathered to do any constructive search in Panama, so I cancelled my flight from the end of May.

Many people – friends and strangers – said that they prayed for a good outcome.

3
THE BREAKTHROUGH

Then, there came a breakthrough. Bill had tried to break into Paul's second email address repeatedly, but he failed to guess the passwords correctly. He contacted Microsoft, but they demanded a Death Certificate for Paul or a Power of Attorney before they could divulge the password. So they refused to help us in any way.

May 22 – Breaking into Paul's second email address.

Finally, however, Bill decided to pretend to be Paul and ask for a new password and guessed the right answers to: sign-in name, address, last sign-in date, approximate date of initial sign-in.

That has changed everything.

There was so much there that it took some days to digest it all. But the basic message was shattering: lots of correspondence till March 7th, and then total silence from Paul. This must mean that he was either dead or captured by guerrillas. We prayed for the latter.

One comfort factor was quickly eliminated. Paul had mentioned that he might join a sailing boat across the Pacific. We found out from his last emails that he had been in contact with the captain and obviously only dilly-dallied with the idea. The new e-mails showed repeated requests from the captain for Paul to join the ship, but no reply from Paul.

So he had not become incommunicado with us because of going on that boat.

May 23

An important thing that the breaking into Paul's Hotmail provided was e-mails showing Paul trying to find a travelling companion "to do the Gap", and a list of further e-mail addresses. Our concern now had to be to find out who his travelling companion was... or if he had one at all.

It took a few days to absorb all these e-mails on Paul's Hotmail sign-on. It seemed Paul has discussed going to the Gap with several people, but none said positively they were going with him. I e-mailed a few of them. He seemed to have contacted a Patricia Upton to see if she knew of others interested in going to the Gap, so I sent her a memo.

We saw emails from his fellow-travellers like these for the period after the silence from Paul from March 7th: "Paul, It's time for a status report from you. April has followed March. How long does this Gap take?" or "Paul, what's up? You don't love me anymore, or have you fallen in love with a monkey, and decided to give up civilization?"

Reading the many memos about the dangers of the Gap from his would-be travelling companions had reinforced our worries.

So what we had to do was to contact everyone that Paul had corresponded with to see if they knew what might have happened or who this Tom was or if Paul definitely went with this companion and a guide.

We found we were emailing people all over the world.

We wondered: what did people in a similar situation do before 1990, when emails came to be available?

There was an email from a Tom Nelson. He turned out to be the lawyer from California, and when we emailed him, he replied saying that he did not go into the Darien Gap with Paul… and of course we got lots of empathy and sympathy from him.

Paul's Fellow Traveller

Bill then picked this single memo out of Paul's Hotmail. It was addressed to a Dickles76, and here was the memo and the reply.

From Paul to Tom: "Good to hear from you. I liked Nicaragua a lot, especially the island on the Lago.

Yes, it is difficult to find others to have a look at the Gap. I know one other English guy who wants to have a look but is undecided at the mo. We can look at it in a rational way, keep going into it, speak to the locals a lot and if it gets too dicey turn back and take the boat. There's a couple of different routes as well, some safer than others. This is a method I've used in other so-called dangerous areas, and it worked.

Currently, I'm in Costa Rica. It's a beautiful place, done some trekking and so on, great cloud forest. Off to Panama tomorrow to scout info for the gap and get some diving done on the Caribbean side.

Enjoy the travels, amigo, and I look forward to having a bash at the gap
with you. Laters,
Paul"

From: "Thomas Hart Dyke" <dickles76@hotmail.com>
To: paulwinder@hotmail.com
Subject: Re: where are you?
Date: Wed, 09 Feb 2000 13:47:19 PST

"DEAR PAUL,
SORRY ABOUT THE DELAY BUT FINDING ONE OF
THESE PLACES ISNT SO EASY NOW. IM IN NICARA-
GUA NEAR THE LAGO DE NICARAGUA AND VERY
INTERESTED IN CROSSING THIS INFAMOUS PLACE.
IM HOT ON YOUR HEELS. FINALLY AFTER A LONG
STALEMATE IN GOOD OLD SAN PEDRO, I'VE TRIED
MY BEST TO PICK UP SOME FOLK ON THE WAY FOR
THE WALK BUT NOT SURPRISINGLY NO-ONES UP
FOR A BITE!!!
I'M READY IF YOU ARE FOR A REALISTIC STAB AT
THIS STROLL, PERO MUCHAS PERSONAS TELL ME
THAT IT REALLY IS A WAR ZONE AND BEST AVOID-
ED, THERE IS A BOAT FROM COLON TO CAREN-
TEGA IN COLOMBIA IF WE DECIDE OTHERWISE.
MARCH 1st WOULD STILL BE VERY CONVIENIENT
PARA MI, SO E -MAIL US A NOTE BACK ON YOUR
LATEST NEWS AND CURRENT THOUGHTS ON THE
SITUATION. MUST DASH AND THE BEST OF LUCK,
    YOUR TRAVELLING FRIEND, TOM."

Bill then sent an email to Dickles76... but got no reply.

So, the name was Tom Hart Dyke. We thought we would
try to follow this lead and find his family.

I went to the Police in Chelmsford to see if they could
tell us how to search for a name in the whole of the UK.
They sent me on to the Library. There I discovered that the

Electoral Registers had recently been put on the Internet, and we would be able to search for the answer ourselves. I discovered that there was a system called 192.com. On first looking into it, there seemed to be no mention of a charge.

We first could only find one Hart Dyke on 192.com, said to live in Station Road in a village near Tunbridge Wells in Kent: no house number given.

One sunny Sunday afternoon, I drove the 50 miles to this rural Kent village and knocked on every door in that long road. When people asked me why I was searching it seemed strange saying, "My son has disappeared in the jungle of Central America 6000 miles away, and his companion may have been a Hart Dyke, living in this road. Do you know anyone of that name?"

I received lots of sympathy at the doors. Then finally I came to a house where the residents said that they had bought the house from the Hart Dykes about 18 months before, and that the Hart Dykes were a married couple aged 40 to 45. So, the husband was not likely to have gone venturing alone around the world. That was obviously not the Hart Dyke I was seeking.

So, we still had not made any contact in the UK with the family of Paul's companion.

More vital advances

The contact that proved most fruitful on Paul's new emails was Patricia Upton. The Upton name had been mentioned before on Paul's other email log-on by Mike Pearson.

Patricia Upton seemingly ran an adventure outfit in the USA, which had some years previously accompanied clients to the Darien. She had stopped that, but she was still greatly interested in the area. She gave lots of names whom I tried to contact in the next few weeks, but I got little information from them... Much activity on my part but no real solutions from most of the contacts.

However Patricia Upton went on to give more useful information when I hinted I might go out to Panama: "Here are some names and contacts that might help you when you get to Panama: Eric Nicolaison, a former marine half-American, half-Panamanian, living in Panama City. Not sure if he will be able to help, but he does know Margarito, who is a very trustworthy Indian guide and dear friend.

Eric should be able to get you in contact with Margarito, but it might take a few days..." and she gave Eric's phone number.

"And there's a hostel in Panama City – the Voyager International Hostel, whose owner is Abdiel O'Callaghan... maybe someone there knows something.

And if you get to the Darien, here's a few names of very trustworthy Indians in Pucuro and Paya along the Darien Gap route."

She also told us that all travel in the Darien was by river and that there were police checkpoints where all travellers had to stop and record their names and passport numbers in a book. The main check-points were at Boca de Cupe and Union Choco on the Tuira river, and also by another river up to Paya near the Colombian border.

She suggested that we should ask the British Embassy to ask the police to check on this.

The only thing that disconcerted me was the motto she quoted after the logo of her adventure outfit. "Life's an adventure… Make it worthwhile": innocent words, but just the kind of words to encourage Paul to make a foolhardy decision.

I phoned Eric Nicolaison at 3 in the morning and introduced myself. From him, we got the suggestion that we could put out a message on a local radio station in Panama City and that it would be heard by the Indians in the Darien area. We tried passing this suggestion on to the British Embassy. They had never heard of the radio station even though it was operating from only a street away from their premises. However, they eventually found it and put out a message on it at a small cost.

The Embassy also took up my suggestion of trying to contact the police station at Yaviza, and asking them to contact the other police stations on the river to see if they knew anything about the two lads logging in. But they got no replies. No wonder. This was 3 months after the lads had passed through, and log-books in those outlying places might not be filed perfectly, and police personnel might have changed.

The Embassy also tried to contact the leader of the LDS American church who had some contact with that jungle area, but he was out of the country.

So all of this was very useful information for my postponed visit to Panama.

We were coming to the conclusion that we no longer needed the British Embassy with its lack of information from official channels or local contacts.

But Patricia Upton passed on to us even more useful information. She had been in correspondence not just with Paul but with a young American called James Spring. It turned out that he had gone through the Darien Gap in January – 2 months before Paul. After coming through at the other end, he had emailed Patricia Upton the following memo of how he had got on.

February 10, 2000

"Dear Mr. & Mrs. Upton,
We made it. We would not do it again – nor would we have done it if we had known the extent of the danger currently afoot in Colombia. We spent 2 days in Pucuro. Juan Rivas, a truly wonderful soul, no longer has the heart or the stomach for travelling beyond Paya.

Nor did anyone else from the village.
My pal and I concocted a way to get to Paya and then inspire a Kuna guide from that village to take us to Palo de las Letras where we would embark solo to Cristales (an abandoned hulk of a village, burnt down by the paramilitaries), build a balsa raft to carry us and our packs at night to Bijao where we would follow a GPS-mandated path to Boca Limon (which still has some villagers).

Everyone – four Panamanian National Police cuartels, the Kuna chief, Gabriel, at Pucuro, and everyone we met – assured us that we would not live to see the Colombian border. Once past Boca de Cupe, we opted to call ourselves French, happy to hide our gringo roots.

The jungle populations are very anti-Colombian paramilitary; a great many are inclined toward the aims of the

FARC. Prior to embarking on this suicide trip from Pucuro, we stumbled across a Colombian who lives in the Colombian village of Arquia, not far from Unguia on a northern arm of the Atrato delta.

He and a friend were returning to their village, over the mountain known as Tugun. He expressed that there would be safety in numbers if he acted as a guide. We passed Paya and scaled the mountain, camping at various clearings including the burned-up village of Payita which was destroyed a year and a half ago by the Colombian paramilitary. The jungle has reclaimed most of the charred remains.

After a few days, we reached the abandoned INDERE-NA station that overlooks the Gulf of Uraba and a day later we reached the Kuna village of Arquia. The next day we travelled solo to Unguia as we could find no one who was not terrified to enter this bastion of renegade paramilitary soldiers.

Along the way we passed through dozens of abandoned fincas, bought back by the Colombian government. We received word of where the paramilitary patrol controlled one side of a low saddle and we stayed far to the other. In Unguia we avoided registering at the Colombian army outpost and caught a private panga to Turbo.

In Pucuro we were told that three Americans had visited 5 months prior and had travelled as far in as Paya before returning and exiting the Darien by air. I can't imagine anyone else being as brainless, obsessed, and fortunate as we were.

Thank you for your helpful advice. It gave us great comfort knowing that even though the playing field had changed much, many players remained the same. Cookie and Estanislao send warm regards...

Best Regards, James Spring."

It seems that Patricia Upton had passed this memo of James Spring onto Paul and that had probably encouraged Paul to think that the Darien Gap was feasible, though dangerous.

So, contacting James Spring was the obvious thing for us to do.

In early June, James Spring emailed us in reply: "Mr. Winder, I was saddened to hear of the disappearance of your son and his friend. I am not sure what sort of assistance I might render, but I assure you that it is offered whole-heartedly in any way you deem necessary. Please feel free to call me at any time," and he gave the phone numbers. "I look forward to speaking with you."

...and he followed it up with another memo, describing his travels and background, but starting off about his worry that he was an element in Paul's disappearing.

"I was sorry to hear that your son and his friend chose to follow our path from Panama into Colombia. I feel a large sense of responsibility – and I have not slept well since reading your first e-mail.

I wish that somebody could have dissuaded your son, Mr. Winder. I truly do. And, while I appreciate what the Uptons have endeavoured to do with their website, the truth of the matter is that the Darien they once traversed a decade ago no longer exists.

Everyone from Kuna elders to Panamanian National Police told us that 10 years ago they would have sent us onward with a blessing and no concerns. But the war has escalated. Things change. And people change."

I would take up contact with James Spring again later.

It was amazing how much people wanted to help.

I have sent an e-mail to my Irish relatives on the basic facts of the case.

I have got an immediate reply from my niece Dana, saying she would accompany me into the Darien – useful because she can speak Spanish more fluently than I. I may take up this offer if I can see precisely what I will do there.

May 26

Anne broke down in church this evening, quietly crying, when someone, in the context of the "Finding in the Temple", spoke about the disappeared of Chile and Argentina. The mere word "disappeared" was enough.

I find that it's only when I have to say the words "It's quite likely that he is dead" that I do the male version of a breakdown – i.e. I am unable to speak for 10 seconds.

Meanwhile, life goes on.

May 27

At the last minute we decided to fly to visit friends in Germany tomorrow as arranged many months ago. This would have been the day I was flying to Panama.

It will be a strain trying to be jolly with friends when our minds are totally preoccupied with trying to find out what has happened to Paul.

May 28

So, we went to the friends in Germany. I found out that

there is internet access at the public library in the village near them. I have visited there to check on my e-mail and getting accustomed to the German keyboard. Our friends think that I am computer-mad just. They did not appreciate why I was doing it. When I broke down about Paul, one of them said: "Oh, yes, we are worried about my 85-year-old mother". They did not realize that the death of a young person (and possibly by violence) is totally different from the death of an older person from natural causes. But I could not blame them: people just don't know how to react and do not realize how the death of a child hits one. I am amazed myself at how much it affects me.

After being stopped in my tracks from going to Panama, here in Germany with poor access to e-mail, we can do even less than at home, and it is frustrating and distressing.

We had learnt a new card game from our friends, but it will always be tarnished by the immense anxiety of this affair.

May 29

Cycling today with our German friends.

But I could not stop thinking of Paul and wanting to be dead too. No wonder people age with the death of their children. In other ways, it is strange: Paul was, of course, different from me as generations are always different. He did not seem to read intellectual books, seemed to have the common young man's love of drinking and of the ephemera of London life, did not love work for itself (as I have always done) but only for the money. But all that does not matter. I greatly miss him, and I mourn the lack of opportunity for him to mature. But we had a shared love of adventure. I felt that dying in me too.

And I could think of nothing but Paul.

I never knew what the "pain of loss" was like until then.

My imagination ran wild on the Paul affair. What had happened? Was Paul captured by revolutionaries? Or by bandits? Or did a guide kill him for the money in his pockets? A few hundred dollars is a lot of money in the Darien, and there are no police in the area to ask questions afterwards. It would be easy to kill with one blow of a machete when a person was asleep at dawn. Or two guides could easily overpower him. Or he could have been carried away by a river. Or they could have got lost: the villages of Cristales and Bijao are burned down, and there are swamps preventing access to the river. What if they came to a burnt-down village and there were no inhabitants and so no dugouts, and they got lost trying to retrace their steps? In the swamps the dugout is the only means of travel.

It was distressing that we might never know what happened.

I thought of the hundreds of thousands "disappeared" or "missing in action" in the First World War, and their family always waiting to find out what happened to them.

And there was the question one cannot suppress.

"Why, why, Paul did you have to go into such extreme danger?"

Even though the answer is obvious, "It would be a good story in the pub when I got back, and an achievement, and I thought my luck would still hold out."

But I noticed that my mind has censured itself from blaming Paul in any way.

4
FRIENDS & STRANGERS RALLY ROUND

I still planned to fly out to Panama.

Meanwhile, the search for the family of Paul's companion, Tom Hart Dyke, continued.

Having been stymied in that attempt on the road near Tunbridge Wells, I then found out that the reason that I had only found one Hart Dyke was that I had not paid a full subscription fee to 192.com. So I paid the subscription fee.

Also a friend, Jenny Gillam, and Kevin, Paul's youngest brother, started making suggestions about the Name HARTDYKE, wild-carding all names starting with HART. The 192 system picked up Hart Dykes with a dash and ones with a space in the middle: HARTDYKE, HART-DYKE and HART DYKE. There were 11 HART-DYKEs, and 38 HART DYKEs. Most of the latter seem to be associated with a chain of shops near Banbury.

But the "HART DYKE" contained just a single Thomas: he was recorded as being, not near Banbury, but near Dartford. I wondered if that is the "Dartford tunnel" in Kent. The exact address turned out to be Lullingstone Castle at the village of Eynsford near Dartford in Kent.

Jenny Gillam found the phone number by rooting through the telephone books in the library. I phoned it.

The man answering confirmed that they had a 24-year-old son travelling in Panama. I was amazed to find that they were not at all worried about their son, despite his not having contacted them for 3 months.

Anne and I planned to visit Lullingstone Castle.

It seemed pretty certain that this was the home of Paul's companion, Tom.

EUREKA, EUREKA, EUREKA!

So that was answer number one question very likely achieved – the identity of Paul's fellow traveller.

We visited the Hart Dykes on June 10th, and it all seemed to fit. The father was Oliver, but was called Guy. The mother was Sarah, the daughter was Anya. Tom has been travelling for 3 years, and his not contacting for 2 months did not cause undue concern.

"Ah, he'll just turn up out of the blue some day," seemed to be Guy's attitude. It was quite different from us who worried.

And I did worry about them because it looked as if they are waiting for Tom to return and take over the running of the stately home. Now there seemed to be a high possibility that he was dead.

We took away a few photographs of Tom, and we saw his cards from Yaviza – rather more informative than Paul's. Tom said the police in Yaviza interrogated them trying to persuade them not to go into the Darien Gap, and that Yaviza was "bristling with arms". He also mentioned a few village names on alternative routes if the "central route" proved too dangerous.

The Hart Dykes had informed the Kent police about the facts, and they police said that they will pass it on to Interpol. But I thought that Interpol would only pass it on to the

Panama police, and from what we'd seen of them so far, nothing will be done by them: the Panama police had Paul's name for 3 weeks by then, and there is no indication that they have enquired of the police posts in the Darien yet.

Tom also didn't mention the name of his companion, but it is obvious that Paul and Tom went together.

We also saw the boxes of seeds sent back from various countries in the world by Tom, a very keen botanist.

The castle grounds and lake of Lullingstone Castle were certainly lovely.

Meanwhile, other contacts were developing

Mid-June:

Patricia Upton kept feeding me other contact information about Panama from her home-base in the USA: Names of various geologists, biologists, church people, also about police check-points on the river, etc. – people I could not easily contact with my poor Spanish and the time-difference of six hours and the limiting consideration that the information from Pat Upton was probably 10 years out of date.

Relatives and friends contributed to the gathering of information.

Jenny Gillam, our friend, was just brimming over with ideas & attempted contacts: with the DAS (Secret police) and the prison system in Columbia, contacting erstwhile-adventure-tour companies in Panama, and the main newspapers in Bogota, and contacting Interpol.

My nephew, Stephen, was engaged in not just running the FINDPAUL website, but also putting a small advert into the newspaper "El Tempo" in Bogota, and on the well-known Lonely-Planet hostel web-site, THE THORN-TREE.

My brother, Percy, contacted the priest who runs a street children's charity in Medellin, which has good contacts there.

Other friends said they were praying for Paul.

As for strangers contacting us, two stood out as leaving us less in the dark at least: Eddie O'Brien, who ran a risk management programme for a multinational company in Bogota and had been out there for 8 years... and Herman, Manager of a very large hikers hostel in Bogota.

Both really came as a result of my nephew, Stephen's, interventions – one from the advert in *El Tempo* and one from the advert in THE THORN-TREE.

Both Eddie O'Brien and Herman contacted other agencies for us, but also gave lengthy explanations of the state of affairs.

Here was Eddie O'Brien's message.

"The countryside is under guerrilla control, and they had their fair share of kidnappings and murders. But the paramilitaries (called ELN) also murdered many people, and they murdered 3 nuns near Turbo just a few months ago and they sabotaged about 250 electricity pylons leading to native villages. There is no police presence in the countryside.

But neither guerrillas nor paramilitaries would gain anything by killing foreigners.

My heart really goes out to you. The uncertainty as to what really happened to Paul and Tom must be terrible. If there is any way I can help, please do not hesitate to contact me."

On the other hand, there was a story from Herman, the manager of the hostel in Bogota.

"Last year three of my guests in Bogota (a Brit, an Israeli and a Swiss girl) bought horses in San Agustin in Colombia to go overland to Ecuador. After 5 days of riding, they got close to the area the government has given to the guerrillas; since paramilitaries have been promising they will send 10,000 armed men to fight the guerrillas, anybody who is not known in the area is considered suspicious of spying for their enemies, the 3 tourists were captured by a FARC commando. They were not handcuffed or mistreated. After 2 weeks the English guy ran away - the other 2 decided to stay thinking it was too dangerous to go into the jungle without equipment. After his escape, the English guy came to Bogota thinking that the other two lives were in danger, and he went to the embassies expecting help but came back very disappointed because of their lack of interest. Meantime, to help them I contacted Fundacion Pais Libre (allied to the paramilitaries) but was disappointed that they were very cautious talking by phone, even though I could speak German with the lady in charge of the Red Cross she gave me an appointment for the week after... that turned out to be pointless because the Israeli and the Swiss were freed by the guerrillas. The guerrillas phoned the bishop from Popayan about delivering the 2 other tourists. The Swiss girl came back to my house and she told us the long story. It´s not that they had fun, but they started teaching English and maths to the guerrillas, had a good relationship with them and considered the whole thing as an interesting experience."

So, his judgement was that tourists should not be a target of the guerrillas or paramilitaries. None of the 5000 tourists who had passed through his hostel had ever been kidnapped. It was all exaggerated in foreign newspapers. The few cases of missing people that he had dealt with had turned out to be travellers who were just too lazy in contacting home and "were found later having fun on a Caribbean beach".

So, the message seemed to be: "Stop worrying."

The British embassies still came up with no information.

And our lack of further information on the Panama side persuaded me to delay the flight to Panama a little more.

5
A VITAL CONTACT, FARC

A friend of our son, Bill, called Chris Taylor had found an Italian source which specialised on providing addresses of rebel groups. They had an email address for FARC, so I sent them an email.

"Señor,

Mi hijo, Pablo Winder, ciudadano ingles – alto, delgado y rubio, tiene 29 Anos – tenia intencion de ir de Yaviza a Colombia atraves de la jungla en marzo – hace tres meses. Era un mochilero que iba a pie.

Ha desaparecido. No sabemos donde se encuentra.

Ruta era tal vez Yaviza, Boca de Cupe, Pucuro, Paya, Paol de las Letros, Cristales, Bijao, Travesia. Pero no estoy seguro.

Alguien en FARC has visto a una persona que responda a esos detailes?

Respeto su causa. Soy Socio de Amnesty International, y ho pedido con frecuencia a Gobierno Colombio clemencia para prisioneros.

Perdon, mi español no es bueno.

Brian Winder."

Which was meant to say: "My son, Paul Winder, an English citizen, tall and slim and fair-skinned, 29 years old, planned to go from Yaviza to Colombia through the jungle in March – 3 months ago. He was a backpacker travelling on foot.

He has disappeared. We do not know what has happened to him.

The route was perhaps Yaviza, Boca de Cupe, Pucuro, Paya, Palo de las Letras, Cristales, Bijao, Travesia. But I am not certain.

Has anyone in FARC seen a person like that?

I respect your cause. I am a member of Amnesty International and I have often pleaded with the Colombian government for clemency for prisoners.

Sorry, my Spanish is not good. Brian Winder."

Of course, I realised that this message would not go to FARC in Colombia, but to a FARC offie in Switzerland, where they had an agent who could operate in freedom and safety.

But I hoped the message would work its way through the chain of command.

I waited and waited.

June 14

I wrote again to FARC, this time with more pleading: "Suplico os, suplico os, decir a me si saben ustedes algo de Paul Winder y su amigo Tom Hart Dyke que salieron de Yaviza en Marzo ir a Colombia atraves de la jungla. No sono Americanos, sono Ingleses.

Paul es mi hijo major. Lloro le.

Eran mochileros, eran muy muy tontos.

Quero solamente saber que ha sucedido.

Respeto su causa. Soy socio de Amnesty International, y he pedido con frecuencia al Gobierno Colombiono clemencia para prisoneros.

Perdon, mi espanol no es bueno.

Responde a esta e-mail direccion, no a Brian Winder, que no travaja."

Translated: "I beg you, I beg you, tell me if you know anything of Paul Winder and his friend Tom Hart Dyke who went from Yaviza in March to go to Colombia through the jungle. They were not Americans, but English.

Paul is my eldest son. I weep for him.

They were back-packers. They were very silly.

I just want to know what has happened.

I respect your cause. I am a member of Amnesty International and I have often written to the Colombian government for mercy for prisoners.

Sorry my Spanish is not good.

Reply to this email address, not to Brian Winder, which does not work."

June 17

At last I have got a reply from FARC, or rather an acknowledgement that they have sent the message on to their operating divisions in Colombia: "Su mensaje lo hemos remitido a nuestra direccion nacional, esperamos alguna respuesta, apenas tengamos alguna razon le transmitiremos. Cordial saludo,

Comision internacional FARC-EP."

Translated: "We have sent your message to our national directorate, and we hope to receive some reply, but we have no evidence to send any message now.

With cordial greetings,

The International Commission of FARC-EP."

It was wonderful getting that message, even though it did not solve the problem immediately.

6
JAMES SPRING & JUNGLE ETIQUETTE

I mentioned already the memo of James Spring to Patricia Upton describing his passing through the Darien Gap and how this had been passed on to Paul.

I decided to send James Spring an e-mail in early July.

I got a reply two days later, explaining again his own journeys and his view of jungle wisdom.

"Mr. Winder, I was saddened to hear of the disappearance of your son and his friend. I am not sure what sort of assistance I might render, but I assure you that it is offered whole-heartedly in any way you deem necessary. Please feel free to call me at any time." And he gave the numbers. "I look forward to speaking with you."

He followed it up with another memo, describing his travels and background, but starting off about his worry that he was an element in my son's disappearing.

Be patient if this repeats some of what he said to Patricia Upton.

"I was sorry to hear that your son and his friend chose to follow our path from Panama into Colombia. I feel a large sense of responsibility – and I have not slept well since reading your first e-mail.

I wish that somebody could have dissuaded your son, Mr. Winder. I truly do. And, while I appreciate what the Uptons have endeavoured to do with their website, the truth of the matter is that the Darien they once traversed a decade ago no longer exists.

Everyone from Kuna elders to Panamanian National Police told us that 10 years ago they would have sent us onward with a blessing and no concerns. But the war has escalated. Things change. And people change.

I have lived much of my adult life in Mexico and Central America. I studied anthropology in the University, and am fluent in Spanish and conversant in many aboriginal languages. I am also a competitive athlete, and prior to our departure to Darien, my pal and I trained hard everyday for months to prepare. Running hills, carrying loads, testing gear. We were still not ready for what the Darien offered us. We also hired a GPS phone not relying on local transmitters but on direct contact to a satellite, a heavy instrument. The one saving grace that I believe delivered us – and the one key that may help you locate your loved ones, rests within a concept too often dismissed by adventurers: cultural sensitivity.

When I read that the Uptons were robbed, and their objects held for ransom by the villagers of Pucuro, I knew that the problem was the level of communication. Prior to departure, I read every anthropological journal ever published on the Kuna and Embera cultures. I knew about the role of the saila, or chief, knew how to approach with humble gifts from my country.

When we were announced within the Gathering Hall of Pucuro and the chief made us wait at the rear until he had finished talking with the village men, we waited. When he spoke to me, I listened, and when I spoke, I exhibited respect and humility. I let him know that I realised we were in his land, and that the key to our successful transit depended upon his wise counsel.

We made many allies this way. But the important thing to note is that any of the allies that I will now name and describe, could, at the drop of a hat, turn and become enemies. I am certain that you have had quite the crash course in Colombian politics, and I apologise for repeating anything that you already know. But I feel it's best to err on the side of caution.

The Kuna Indians live in a communal society. They share labour and pool resources. The fruits of their efforts are distributed equally among all members of the village. The Colombian FARC rebels have communist aims. Remember, the rebels are not highly trained mercenaries, they are peasants fighting for a cause that they believe to be equality. Their ranks are comprised of humble villagers – and Indians who are already pre-disposed to cling to the precept of equal work, equal rewards.

As such, the Kuna Indians of the Darien are natural targets for the Colombian paramilitary, a force that we had vastly underestimated until our arrival in the jungle. Right-wing paramilitary forces have tortured a great many Kuna Indians and destroyed their villages. As such, the Kuna feel threatened on every front. The chiefs use this information as fear to keep a tighter rule over their people. Kuna Indians do not enjoy free movement between villages. Sometimes, when the hierarchy of power is breached by an outsider, the Kuna chiefs or ranking villagers will make an example of the offender.

The three missionaries that were killed in Pucuro, the Uptons troubles in the same village are all examples of this. Five months prior to our crossing, three Americans endeavoured to do the same but were forced to return from Paya. There is no continuing through the jungle without the blessing of the chief. They will find you.

Sadly, this is not the primary threat to life and health in the Darien. That honour belongs to the paramilitary. The old maps of the area show a prominent village called Cristales, now completely disappeared. The previous trail from Panama to Colombia's Boca Limon is now abandoned and overgrown. The paramilitary is said to maintain a strong presence in the area. We planned to attempt a night crossing by following GPS co-ordinates to Palo de las Letras and the ruins of Cristales, and, there, build a raft that would float us to Bijao. We felt that the night crossing would let us see the fires of the paramilitary camps, and avoid detection.

Three hours before we endeavoured to do this, luck shined on us. I must sound arrogant when talking of the preparations in which we invested. I realize, more than anyone, that the thing that delivered us safely to Colombia was a fortunate roll of the dice. That roll, for us, came in the form of a merchant named Albero.

Albero, and his friend Eliseo, are currently residents of the Colombian Kuna village of Arquia (in Colombia, a day's journey by foot onward from Unguia).

I say "currently" because neither of these men are Kuna. Albero's family's ranch was in the hills above Arquia, but the farm was abandoned due to the encroachment of the paramilitary forces who have monopolized the territory. Today, 27-year-old Albero, makes his living by buying first-world goods: envelopes of hot cocoa, bras, panties, and other lightweight fare which he then carries across the mountains to the Kuna villages as far away as Pucuro. There he sells the items, often clearing $200 (US) for each trip. (The Kuna have a small amount of currency as a result of harvest surplus which is sometimes taken by pirogue to Panama's river-front villages for sale to non-Kuna.)

Albero, Eliseo, and a skinny dog named Llanero were heading back to Arquia the next morning. They invited us along. Albero said that there was safety in numbers. But I knew what he was thinking. He was thinking that the paramilitary would let them pass unmolested because we had American-looking gringos in tow (It is widely believed that the USA is a major source of the paramilitary's arms and funding.)

The problem with the new path was that, rather than allowing us to cross in the low saddle of the mountain range that separates Panama from Colombia, we would have to scale the peak known as El Tugun.

We felt we had little choice. We left the next morning. After a couple of days on the trail guided fairly expertly by Albero, we only had to consult the GPS once to get us back on the path, we came upon the former village of Payita on the Rio Payita. A year-and-a-half earlier, Payita was a thriving Kuna paradise of domesticated banana and sugar cane fields. Today it is a burned-out reminder of the nefarious aims of the paramilitary. Only charred posts remain. It is said that the paramilitary (largely consisting of Colombian army soldiers) tortured the Payita Kuna and destroyed the village for aiding the FARC rebels. A Sergeant Ramos, based in Unguia, is reported to be the one who led the campaign.

At the Alto de Limon, along the official boundary with Colombia, we were able to see to the Caribbean. We also saw the abandoned farms that stretched from the base of the mountain to the hill that obscured our view of Arquia

On the back side of the obstructing hill is a major base for paramilitary forces. Albero and Eliseo were very nervous going through here. We lay low and stayed off any paths. That night, we were well received in the village of Arquia by the friendly Kuna and their chief. We thanked Albero and Eliseo profusely for their assistance in delivering us to Colombia. We paid them a couple of hundred dollars. They thanked us and reminded me that we were not home yet. We still had to get to Unguia. They could not go into Unguia. Albero asked that I not mention his name there. He'd had problems with the paramilitaries in the past.

The Chief offered to guide us a third of the way to Unguia the next morning. We agreed on a price of $5. We camped beside Albero and Eliseo that night and rose at 4:00 am to walk to the chief's house. We walked in the rain for two hours until the chief stopped and said, I go no further. We thanked him and followed the path three more hours to Unguia. It was not until we reached Unguia that we realized we had been robbed by our dear guides Albero and Eliseo – insignificant stuff, really. Swiss army knife, MagLite. Still a cheap price to pay, obviously.

Unguia is a tough town. The Colombian Army exhibits a huge show of force. At night, the soldiers take off their uniforms and torture peasants. We decided not to sign in at the checkpoint as required. Instead, we hired a private panga to take us across the Gulf of Uraba to Turbo and registered there.

I am sorry to make your acquaintance under these circumstances. I am also sorry for the role that I may have inadvertently played in the events leading to your son's belief that the path to Unguia was a safe bet. I wish that there was something that I could do to take it all back.

In Colombia, there are no safe bets. Anybody that I mentioned to be an amiable resource, could also be a mortal enemy.

Please feel free to contact me by telephone or by this e-mail address at any time. The offer is also extended to the Hart Dyke family."

These were extraordinary intimate revelations from a total stranger, and I felt that we had, at last, an ally.

7

THE SEARCH IN PANAMA

With this extra information from Patricia Upton, James Spring and others, it seemed to be now time to visit Panama and I started preparing for it. I swatted up my Spanish. I bought purifying tablets for the jungle and made enquiries about mobile phones. It seemed that in the jungle one would need to have the old cumbersome type that directly contacted the satellites, which are very costly, so I gave up.

I booked the flight for 15th June.

I prepared a dozen laminated sheets with Paul and Tom's photos with the text, "Desaparecido 10-20 marzo" and the likely route, "Boca de Cupe, Pucuro, Paya, Cristales, Bijao, Travesia" or "Paya, Unguia". The idea is to hand these out in the villages: the lamination will protect them from the damp of the jungle.

I also laminated my list of e-mail addresses and phone numbers. There are two pages of addresses by now.

I also did a rapid update of my will.

I again phoned Eric Nicolaison in Panama City from the UK and said I was flying out.

June 15

I flew out to Panama.

Anne dropped me with many hugs and some tears at Gants Hill to go for the Heathrow flight. I spent the whole of the flight swatting up my Spanish. So I was somewhat exhausted from the 32 hour day.

I turned off the air-conditioning in the hotel in Panama City, so as to get used to the heat for going down the Darien.

June 16

First thing in the morning I phoned Eric Nicolaison and took a taxi out to his place. The houses are all well-defended in that suburb of Panama City – with high walls and razor wire and alarms. Eric was very hospitable and provided lunch. He speaks both Spanish and English fluently. We studied maps, and I showed him my laminated sheet with the photos of the lads to help me in the search. He told me of his journey down the Darien with Patricia Upton, and how a Canadian in the party was left guarding a broken down vehicle. He was murdered and the vehicle was stripped. But it was rather silly to leave a person on his own in the jungle.

All this added to my feeling of insecurity.

We went in his vehicle to find the Indian Margarito in another suburb – a little shanty town by a river. We approached down a dirt track and stopped outside a tiny house on stilts. The Indian, unlike others on the same site, had built his house on 6 foot concrete stilts since the river overflows every year and floods all the other houses: wise fellow. We got out of the car and looked up the ladder to this tiny wooden house where the Indian lay at the door with his sister's three kids peering down at us. However, with the house on stilts the Indian said that he took the precaution of having a metal sheet under him at night in case anyone sticks a machete through the floorboards to kill him.

On the security situation, Eric told me how Margarito had decided to have a party with some neighbours a few years ago, and his part was to bring a chicken. So, he was walking back home along the main road swinging his chicken, and a person from a passing truck hit him on the head with a beer bottle. When he woke up, he had a slash in his head, but he had no chicken, no shirt and no trousers. An interesting story.

So we sat on rocks under a tree in his tiny garden, and Eric told the story of my son having disappeared, and he asked if Margarito would act as my guide in the Darien: all this in Spanish.

But there was a problem: Margarito had a weekend job now and couldn't be absent because he might never get another job in his life. So, he could only fit in an expedition between Monday morning and Friday midday. We spent 2 hours discussing how he could fit it in without missing his work, and how I could get him to the airport at the correct time, and collect him, and what it would cost since everything is expensive in the remote Darien especially if you need to travel at speed.

Margarito was illiterate and that was something of a disadvantage. But he understands numbers.

I suggested that I go down to Yaviza with him, and do some enquiries there myself while he went up the trail, but he said that word would get around that he had come down with a white man, and peoples lips would close. So he said I must remain in Panama City.

We then agreed on what the trip might cost, and where I could pick him up at midnight after he had finished his parking warden shift in the city centre car park, then put him onto a plane for El Real in the Darien on Monday morning.

I still judged it was worthwhile trying to use him thus, simply because there was no-one else, and because the Panama police had been silent since the British Embassy had asked them for information 3 weeks ago: information that they certainly had – the sign-ins of the lads on the police-posts on the Tuira river.

June 17

So I was excluded from the trip down the Darien. I got the money out to give to Margarito, and selected out some equipment that would help him – an umbrella, and water purifying tablets. I have booked the airplane – only $34 each way.

june 18

I wandered around Panama City on foot. Even the rough areas didn't seem as bad as it was made out to be – but I kept my eyes skinned. I looked around the hotel where Paul had stayed in the San Felipe district.

The hotel I had booked into had email, so I could occupy myself a little at that.

June 19

It all worked with my Indian.

With a certain amount of apprehension, I went out into the nearly deserted streets in the middle of the night, took a taxi and I picked up Margarito where he was finishing his shift at 12.30 midnight near the centre of the city, brought him back in a taxi to my hotel where we slept, and brought him out to the airport this morning to fly to El Real in the Darien. He carried pictures of Paul and Tom.

June 21

It was boring, hanging around Panama City. I would far prefer to be in the Darien jungle.

June 23

I went to the airport around midday and found Eric Nicolaison there also – out of the generosity of his heart; I had
been going to collect Margarito and take a taxi out to Eric's
place. We collected Margarito from the plane, and brought
him to Eric's place to debrief him.

Debriefing him was a wonderful experience, because he
acted everything out dramatically, and the maps he drew
were extraordinary sketched out on the veranda floor.

Margarito had only managed to get to Pucuro.

At first, the people he asked in El Real, Yaviza, Boca
de Cupe and Basal all denied that they had seen the two
lads. He asked at 3 police-stations and they all said that
they knew nothing; most of them said that they hadn't been
there in March.

But finally he did come across a person who remembered
seeing two white young men between El Real and Boca de
Cupe, then he went up to the village of Pucuro, and four people there remembered seeing them, and some of them said a
black boatman had poled them up the river to Pucuro. Others had seen the lads going off towards Paya in the morning
without a guide. Perhaps the reason that they hadn't taken
a guide was because the Indians of one or the other villages
had a monopoly on being guides. Some had seen armed men
setting off in the same direction half an hour later.

The main point, however, was that Margarito did not get to
Paya in the scheduled time because it would have involved
an overland journey of a day to get to the river for Paya. So,
we did not know whether the lads had disappeared before or

after Paya (effectively whether in Panama or in Colombia) and what route the lads took after Paya – South or East. So I judged it best to ask the Indian to go up the trail again on the following Monday with instructions to go straight up to Paya by river.

I would again, like last week, be able to collect him at his car park at midnight on Sunday night, and bring him to the airport on Monday morning, before I flew back home on Tuesday. I asked Eric Nicolaison if he would collect him at the airport and debrief him on the Friday afterwards, and I would get the findings over the phone from Eric.

June 24

It was very frustrating to use Internet in Panama. It constantly went down, and I lost all my typing. This was after I had overcome the problems of the Spanish keyboard with my touch-typing.

The 4 pm downpours occurred every day.

June 26

It all worked again. I collected Margarito in the night from his car park, brought him to the hotel, and in the morning brought him to the airport for the flight to El Real.

I met Andy at the British Embassy, and found out that it was only by the British consul mentioning it in a meeting with the chief of police was it revealed that the lad's names had been recorded at the police post at Boca de Cupe. It is like getting blood out of a stone to get any information from the Panamanian police. No word about entries in police books at other points on the river or the exact dates.

The police must know some rumour about what has happened to the lads. The Indians thought that there is a secret pact between the police and the Colombian guerrillas – a kind of "live and let live" policy. It would be reasonable since individuals on both sides don't want to be killed.

A disadvantage of using Margarito was that he has no authority. So he was not allowed access to the police books on the river. But who else could I use, if the police wouldn't cooperate?

June 27

I flew home from Panama.

When I found that I had to transfer between airports in New York to travel on to London on the way home, the customs guard noticed I didn't have my own passport, but instead the passport of my middle son when he was 2 years old with a photograph which was very definitely not of me. However, I just said to the US border officials that they would have had to feed me if they locked me up, so they might as well let me change airports and fly home to London.

I would have been very different after 9-11.

Yes, I suppose I had been suffering from stress in my preparations to travel.

Just about this time, I began to understand better the social situation in Panama and Colombia

One thing I heard from Margarito was about Pat Upton. Seemingly she brought a motorbike up to Pucuro some years ago, and when she woke up the next morning, she found that Indians had surrounded it and demanded $600 as a release fee. She eventually had to pay half that amount, but this obviously demonstrated what James Spring had said: a friend at one time can easily turn into an enemy later on if one does not observe the correct etiquette.

She had also stayed in the village of Balsal. It is said to be a settlement founded by ex-slaves who had run away from the plantations in the last century. She only stayed one night there, but two nights after she left, the village was surrounded by hundreds of heavily armed guerrillas who had come, the Indians said, specifically to kill her. They don't want white people there, especially Americans. She had probably never heard of this fact because she had already gone away when the guerrillas arrived. A narrow escape.

July 1

I phoned Eric Nicolaison at 3 am from the UK, and got the news from the debriefing.

The Indian had said the following: the lads had slept in Paya, and on the morning afterwards had set out east, which would take them to Payita (burnt-out by the paramilitaries a year ago) and eventually Arquia and Unguia, and then across the bay to Turbo.

With them were two guides, who were Colombians, who had come up with them from the Boco de Cupe. The Indians do not trust these people who drift in from Colombia: no-one dares ask them where they have come from or who they are.

The Indian chief in Paya and the person who does the immigration formalities there warned the two lads that they should not go beyond Paya, especially with the Colombian guides. There is a high likelihood that Paul's Spanish was not good enough to understand the warnings.

Nothing is known after that.

No-one knew the names of the guides. One doesn't dare ask names.

Conclusion: so, the lads disappeared between Paya and Turbo.

8
A CONFUSION OF CONTACTS

June to July

When I came back from Panama I thought that the only way forward now was to see if we could find someone who had an expert knowledge of the area. There were e-mails every day following up leads, but no real information. E-mails, after all, are sent by people who live in cities. There is no contact between that world and the world of the jungle.

I was commuting on the M25 for an hour to work & back at the time, and as I drove I had two repeating hallucinations – both involuntary – one was of Paul being murdered in the forest by robbers or revolutionaries and his body left there, the other of my coming home and as I entered the front door, the phone ringing, and my going to it and hearing, "It's Paul. I'm OK." Then I would wake out of the dream (a bit dangerous on the M25) and know that I would never see Paul again. And I would come home to Anne and tell her, and we would both cry.

We, of course, talked of selling the house if Paul was in the hands of guerrillas and a ransom demand was made.

But the search went on.
Where to turn next was the problem.
It would be a very rare person in the English-speaking world who would know this Spanish-speaking area of Central America, and especially know its jungle area.

It would need the widest possible publicity to find a person with contacts there. I decided on an article in the Times. I gathered together material for one.

July 2

I e-mailed Patricia Upton what I have found out so far – that the lads had travelled East from Paya.

It seemed that the search must switch to the Colombian side now. The lads could have got as far as Unguia, and then disappeared after that.

I had e-mailed Fra Gabriel in Colombia what I had discovered from my Indian: that Paul and Tom had disappeared between Paya and Unguia, and that they had two Colombian guides with them. Fra Gabriel had arranged for a message to be put out on the radio in Colombia, which the guerrillas might hear. He had also sent a message to the bishops in that area, and I believe spoken on one of those TV programmes in Colombia which are totally dedicated to kidnap victims. Such a programme would be shown a few times on TV.

I was getting quite accustomed to e-mailing in Spanish – though I don't know what the people at the other end thought of it.

Perhaps I should explain that I first heard of Fra Gabriel as a missionary in Mozambique. A Mozambiquan refugee called Lopez Quichine in England and myself had set up a charity to build schools in Mozambique and had gathered funds for that in England. Fra Gabriel was a Franciscan missionary in Mozambique who was part of the chain of intermediaries enabling 5 separate schools to be built with our funds including one major secondary school. He had since returned to Colombia, his native country.

Lonely Planet

I put an entry on the "Thorn Tree" Lonely Planet site warning about the Darien Gap. I put the message more starkly, "Don't, don't, don't go into the Darien Gap. It is certain death." I left it to others to qualify that.

I also asked the Lonely Planet books to revise their narrative on the Darien area of Panama so as not even to mention the route from Yaviza to Colombia. This seemed far better than mentioning it giving warnings, because some foolhardy young man would ignore the warnings. I told them all briefly of the Paul incident, and about James Spring and what had happened to Patricia Upton.

July 3

Bill had e-mailed all the people on Paul's address list, explaining that he has broken into Paul's Hotmail, and found that Paul hadn't accessed it since early March. He then told them the basic story of the search. "However, the trail has gone dead, as it appears that Paul and Tom went into an area that even the local people are afraid to enter."

July 4

Another of Paul's correspondents has offered to help find the e-mail address of ELN and the paramilitaries, the AUC or PAISLIBRE (all seemingly the political front for the paramilitaries).

I already have the Internet site or homepage, but do not know the e-mail address.

The website of PAISLIBRE or COLOMBIALIBRE were very impressive propaganda – how they want everyone to live in peace and freedom. Very different from some of the paramilitaries activities, where they murdered nuns and torture Indians and burn down their villages.. In war often the extremists prevail.

I wrote to them both in Spanish with a message similar to the FARC message.

COLOMBIALIBRE replied in Spanish but also translated it.
"Mr. Brian Winder,
Receive a cordial greeting.
We regret their situation. In the area where you inform us that the facts happened it operates a guerilla front of the FARC.
We will try to communicate with our men in the I Choco to investigate if they are informed of some kidnapping of foreigners carried out by the guerillas fighters of the FARC that operate between the bordering area of Panama and Unguia in the I Choco. Cordially, Leonardo.
Relate Public AUC."

July 5

Patricia Upton replied to my most recent email: she was busy in the middle of her holiday season, since she runs a back-of-beyond camp.
She also gave some other possible contacts: (1) a Rob Lambert who had tried to travel from Unguia to Panama two years ago, but had been stopped by the Colombian army at Unguia, and forced to go by boat along the coast, (2) an

employee of the National Parks of Colombia in Turbo in the mid-80's (!), (3) the director of the National Parks in Bogota and Medellin and (4) a Francisco Ramos, who she describes as having a ranch near Turbo.

Very kind of her to give me these contacts, but some of them seem a bit out of date and dodgy: Francisco Ramos was head of one group of paramilitarie, and it would be inadvisable to contact him.

I asked the British Embassy again if they had any contacts in Unguia – the place where James Spring's guides ended up. But it is very unlikely. They said no, which was reasonable since Unguia was in Colombia.

July 6

I tried all of the Colombian side contacts provided by Patricia Upton, but failed to find anyone who replied: all the phone numbers were out of date.

I tried hard to find out Francisco Ramos' phone number. I tried in the Colombian embassy in London. I asked Juan Martin – the Colombian archaeologist working in Panama – and he asked a friend in Medellin to look it up, but when he did get a number it only left me with the dilemma of deciding whether to phone in the middle of the night and give a complicated message in Spanish. My Spanish isn't up to that, and I can't drag a friend around at 1 am to do the translating.

Internet is amazing: I contact a person like Juan Martin without knowing where he actually is, and I ask him to help me a total stranger... and he goes to a lot of trouble in doing so.

9
IS THERE AN END TO THE RAINBOW?

I wonder if you, dear reader, are getting bored with the galaxy of contacts that seem to lead nowhere.

I now wonder if, at the time, I was suffering from Obsessive Compulsive Disorder that made me follow every possible lead to the pot of gold of finding my son.

Or was hyperactivity a substitute for worrying or despairing?

If you are bored with too much detail, dear reader, just skip this chapter!

July 6

A list of names contacting me and asking if they could help slips off the tongue: Juan Martin, Christina Barber, Veronique, Lucia Martinez, Susanna Rance, Sarah de Jong, Tamir Betese, Anna Nystrom, Joyce Marie, Ravi Kapur, Stephanie Duchiron, Ben Kohn, Nick Morathon, Mike Ferrante, Lynne of Oxfam, Deborah of Arizona, Tim Wyma – who had been back-packers in Panama but located in different areas of the world now. Names held in mind in case just one could provide some vital piece of evidence.

Another possible lead for information came up, and I followed it because it was in the region where Paul and Tom would have ended up if they had got through the Darien Gap.

Here is the story.

My nephew, Kieran, contacted a journalist friend on the Irish Independent newspaper, called Karl McGinty, who somehow or other knew of an eco-village near Unguia in Columbia.

That is the area where Paul and Tom would have ended up if they had gone through the Gap successfully.

The eco-village was called variously La Caravana or the Darien Foundation or Empressas Solidarias de Salud de Unguia. It was set up by an organisation based in Tennessee USA called ENA. Its object was entirely non-political – with the sole object of cultural exchange and education. It was at Trigana bay near Unguia.

Unguia had another advantage: it has a Red Cross post, and had in the past had Peace Brigades and Justice & Peace Groups visiting it.

Various people associated with the eco-village were very co-operative in answering emails: Liora Adler, Claudio Madaune were some, the latter being the leader who had spent 15 years setting up the eco-village.

However, the most useful contact was Mario Medina who was born in Unguia, and who in adult life had been the only democratically elected mayor that Unguia had ever had – before the paramilitaries deposed him.

Of course, the whole province was an area of unrest and danger, as a result of the government or paramilitaries driving Indians off their ancestral land and murdering them if they tried to come back and bombing their villages from helicopters.

It transpired in the end that even Mario Medina was not able to find out anything about Paul or Tom.

July 7

Among those who replied to Bill's memo there was one of Paul's acquaintances whose ex-wife had 3 uncles high up in the Colombian army. He offered to get a message through to them to see if they could initiate any enquiries. The problem is that they are all located near Bogota. "This may seem to be clutching at straws, but I imagine you would welcome any straws at the moment. We are all very shocked here". So I told him the basic facts of the case to pass on.

July 8

The Hart Dykes had phoned me up and said that they don't want any article in the newspapers. When I had mentioned the possibility to them a few weeks ago they thought it was a good idea, and laid down only one condition – that their name be spelt with a space in the middle. Now they didn't want their names mentioned at all: a complete change in mid-course.

I was now worried about the Indians of Paya: were Paul and Tom so bad mannered to them when they stayed in their village that the Indians decided that they were tired of foreigners visiting them and arranged to have them murdered. After all, something like that is quite possibly what happened to the three missionaries who disappeared in 1994. The lads using Colombian guides instead of Kuna guides would also have been an insult to the Indians.

July 9

The guy whose wife had three uncles in the Colombian

army did speak to his mother-in-law in Bogota about Paul and Tom. She said she would mention it to her brothers. However, I am doubtful if it will help, and I've said to Paul's friend: "Thanks for your trouble. I think we will leave it for the moment. The reason is that if the Colombian army got involved, by the time the message got to Turbo and Unguia, it would be handed over to the paramilitaries (equals the army with their uniforms off), and they would only torture and kill Indians who had nothing to do with the incident. Even the possibility of that is too high a price to pay."

But I didn't like putting people off like this because there is such kindness and goodwill.

More research on the internet unearthed a many-page memo from a volunteer who had spent a year in Turbo. Justice and Peace sponsored him. He seems to know the area well, and is very articulate. He might be an ideal contact if he is still there. I e-mailed him.

July 13

Eddie O'Brien suggested putting a radio message out on the Colombian side. It was a good idea, but I thought I would rely on Fra Gabriel's efforts in this direction.

July 14

The Hart Dykes said that they have been recommended a good detective Agency in Bogota. Sarah Hart Dyke is going out next weekend to see what she can stir up in Colombia in the search for information.

July 15

The company I was working for near London had been

merged with another, farther away. I would then have to drive 90 miles to work and back. So I decided to drop down to working only 2 days a week instead of 5. No harm, because this searching for Paul was taking up much of my time.

July 19

Sarah Hart Dyke had gone out to Bogota and seemed to be incommunicado there. The press kept ringing us up, even from Bogota, trying to locate her, but we could not help.

Since they came back with no information, this was quite likely to be the end of this line of enquiry.

July 20

I still followed up the British Embassy in Panama – but they have got no information from the Panama police. The police can't even tell if the lads' names were recorded in the books at Yaviza, Vista Alegre or Union Choco on the rivers, or at Puerto Obaldia on the Atlantic. It is such a simple task to look for names in a book on specific days. The request for information has been with them for over 5 weeks, and no reply except the one entry at Boca de Cupe, which the British Ambassador wangled out of the chief of police through a personal interview. It was as if the Panamanian police were there to conceal information rather than provide it.

The Embassy rep seemed to actually welcome the article in the *Sunday Telegraph*. He said that Reuters have phoned him, and that an article will appear in the Panamanian press. This must put pressure on the police to provide some information. Or would it?

Strange, I had never been in a situation like this before, but I thought the British Embassy might not welcome press articles. Perhaps I am influenced by the Hart Dykes who dislike the press and all open information. It was good to see the British Embassy's attitude.

We had also been asking the Embassy to press for information about the two guides that the lads picked up in Boca de Cupe. But that would involve intelligence work by the Panamanian police and I did not seriously expect any results from that. But the names of the guides should be recorded beside the lads' names at Boca de Cupe at least.

Of course, the British Embassy was in a hopeless position, being confined to Panama City and with no direct contact, and having to move through official channels only. And it has very few staff.

At first, I was impressed by them and thought that they could do something. Then I realized they were almost powerless.

July 23

The missionary in Colombia Fra Gabriel suggested that we take advantage of the peace talks in Geneva between the Colombian Government and the guerrillas.

I thought that it is a bit of a way-out idea, since the peace talks are about momentous national decisions, and we should not be distracting them with trivial incidents like that of Paul and Tom.

July 24

The Australian Justice and Peace volunteer had not replied. The internet is strange. You have people putting very voluble and articulate memos on, and when one e-mails them, there is total silence and no reply. It's as if people said, "I'm going to be articulate now and never again." So that was the end of that line of investigation.

10
QUITE LIKE OBITUARIES

July 6

Lots of replies have come back from Paul's friends as a result of Bill's e-mail of two days ago. Most had a similar message: "I don't really know what to say. Paul is a good friend.
To say I was shocked and distressed is putting it mildly."

"I was very shocked and so sorry to hear this news... but
don't lose hope."

"What worrying news. You, your family and Tom's are
in my thoughts, and I hope you get some good news soon."

"I had been asking whether anyone had heard anything
from Paul since my last e-mail in March... This must be
a trying and deeply upsetting time for all your family. It's
clear to me that he is a person of great resilience and mental
strength, and let us all trust that he may yet endure. Please
keep me posted."

"I'm really at a loss for words about Paul and his friend. I
just can't believe it."

"For the brief period I got to know Paul I found him great
company and a fascinating guy".

Then from a girl, Ayano Higashiyama, looking up her
Japanese-English dictionary: "When I first saw the name of

Paul on my Hotmail, I was happy, because I worried about him, because he had never sent me e-mail since the last one from Panama City – before he went into the jungle. With being happy I opened your e-mail. Then I was afraid to read it.

I read your e-mail with a dictionary now, and I mail you though I have no idea what I am going to write to you.

Paul and I met at Creel in Mexico first... then we met again at youth hostel in Oaxaca...

Then I didn't see him again, but when I was in Pedro La Laguna, in Guatemala, I saw a friend who had met Paul and Tom there. Paul and my friend had been studying at the Spanish school and spending Christmas there. Paul had already left when I came so I could not see him.

We had a great time together in Mexico. We talked a lot. He told me about his first trip to Africa. It was very interesting for me. He was born and spent his first 6 years in Africa. And we talked about life....

He was also telling me about the plan to cross the jungle between Panama and Colombia. He was so excited. When I met him the second time he told me he had found someone to accompany him. It was Tom. I didn't know the name but I found that he was also English.

I was very interested in the jungle trip and I wanted to go, but I was afraid about robbers, dangerous animals, and also myself. I didn't have enough power to walk with my heavy backpack for more than 1 week. So I gave up the idea. He knows how interested in it I was. He promised to tell me about his jungle trip. We were really good friends.

I can't believe that he is missing now. I don't want to believe it. My English is not good, but even in Japanese I have no idea how I can tell you my feeling. I can just tell you that I am believing in Paul, and I wait for something from him.

He is a very brave guy, and I liked him very much. I hope with you for his safety. I really want to see him."

And then another quite fulsome one: "What terrible news. I feel very sad.

I met Paul in San Ignacio (Belize), and also at Lake Atitilan (Guatemala) on Christmas Day 1999. We did some trekking together around the lake and on one of the volcanoes there. Paul was a great travelling companion and very happy in what he was doing.

I was with Paul when we met Tom at a bar in a town on the side of Lake Atitilan (I think it was called San Pedro, below the volcano of the same name). We were having a few beers after the trek on the volcano. Paul mentioned his plan to do the trip across the Darian Gap and Tom made Paul promise to get in touch later as Tom also wanted to do that crossing to Colombia. Tom had been learning Spanish in the village for some time. He was incredibly enthusiastic about trees, particularly Eucalyptus trees... a real passion."

Quite like obituaries – all rather choking stuff.

11
JAMES SPRING MAKES CONTACT AGAIN

July 10

James Spring had followed with another memo, and seemed to be getting more interested in the case. This was different from the many others who took a brief interest and then gave up. I told my brother that we had at last found a contact who might be able to get us closer to the action.

James Spring's e-mail said: "Thank you for your kind e-mail. I know that this must be an angst-filled time. Sorrow and anger and frustration don't bake well together. I know that I feel only a tiny fraction of what you are going through, but it is enough to make me sad and angry, too.

If the Hart Dykes are thinking of going to Colombia, please show them my memos to warn them of the danger.

I believe Albero & Eliseo to be important keys to finding info, whether they share guilt or not (and I'm not making a judgement here).

Here's what I would do: fly two men into Cartagena, then to Turbo. Bogota is as far from the Darïen as London, as far as information is concerned. Going there is no use. Start at Turbo.

Rent a boat to Unguia, arriving at dusk. Avoid detection; don't sign in. Travel under cover of darkness to the Kuna village of Arquia, using GPS coordinates.

In Arquia, find the chief. Find out if your son arrived in Arquia. If so, return to Unguia, check the registry there. There is much violence in Unguia. If your son did not arrive in Arquia, garner his protection and blessing. Have him stay beside you as you seek Albero and Eliseo, checking first at the hut of Felipe. Albero often camps out back. Maintain "watches" while camped.

If Albero is there and knows nothing, hire him to take you up the mountain to the abandoned village of Payita. This is a day-trip for the paramilitary. It is the most likely place that your son would have stumbled upon either FARC or paramilitary. Payita is two days hike from Paya. Search the small village for signs. Do you know what type (or colours) of gear or possessions that your son carried? Food, wrappers, toilet paper? There are a couple of cleared out areas in Payita where setting up camp is most viable.

If the disappearance was wrought at the hands of man, I believe that the two-day area between Unguia and Payita will be the most likely source of answers.

If not, if your son disappeared before Payita, he may have been followed from either the Kuna village of Pucuro or Paya.

Did Paul leave Paya with guides? If so, where are these guides now? From which village did they come originally? Were they Kuna?

If Paul and his friend went without guides, were they in strong physical condition? Did they carry a GPS receiver? Had they been in the jungle before? Did they pack Oral Rehydration Salts? Were they happy enough with their lives in the UK?

It is the middle of the rainy season. Remember, extra precautions must be taken.

I believe that answers can be found if you are committed to seeking them. But maybe the answers themselves are not so important. Maybe it is the lessons that are important at this point. And those can be learned without a trip into Darien.

I hope that you find whatever it is that you seek and wish you the very best."

My reaction to this extraordinary memo was that this is precisely what I would do if Anne wasn't so worried about losing me. James Spring has outlined with extreme clarity and with lots of information where the answers may be found... but Anne would worry too much if I went missing... This was a problem.

July 11

I e-mailed James Spring back, telling him not to worry – that I doubt if Paul was encouraged by James' success in getting through, but that it was sheer love of adventure that drove Paul on

"Dear James,
Just to answer some of your questions for curiosity.
On the other question of deciding what I am to do, that'll take longer, since my wife doesn't want to lose me too.

GUIDES: They picked up two guides in Boca de Cupe (the Indians of Paya classed these as Colombians and were very distrustful of them), and the lads proceeded with these guides beyond Paya. They probably had no idea of how much this would offend the Indians in Paya... and I doubt if they showed the Indians in Paya the civility you talk about... that's the problem with the Lonely Planet books – they give very superficial guidance on culture.

I have asked the British Embassy in Panama to get the

police to find out who these guides were – but you know the Panama police: they wouldn't know where to start doing this. (Would you know: would the guides also have had to write their name in the Police book, say at Boca de Cupe, as well as the whites?)

You ask if Paul and Tom were happy?
Paul: Yes... but he did live for these 5-month journeys in between 18-month bouts of city working (previous 2 trips, Africa and the East).
Tom (a guess): his parents have a stately home, and I suppose his travels were an adventure before settling down to the sedentary life of showing people around the stately home. After all, anyone who does anything can be said to be 'unhappy' with what they did before; that's why they changed what they were doing.

Do not fear, I never mind questions: openness and truth and the curious paradoxes of life interest me. Secrecy is alien to me.

But remember, we had to discover all this – even whether he had a companion at all, and who that companion was (done by searching voter's lists) – by breaking into Paul's Hotmail and sending memos all over the world; after that, I had to spend two weeks in Panama to discover that he reached Paya and went East from it.
Up to the point of breaking into his Hotmail (Microsoft were fussy about it, and my other son had to pretend he was Paul and guess at the answers), where exactly he was going was only known from an e-mail to his brother – not to us – on 8th March, and a postcard to us from Yaviza. The implications of it I did not realise at that time, but it would have been too late anyway.

It has been a pretty exhausting 7-weeks since we started the investigations.

Thanks for your kind interest."

July 12

James Spring replied:

"I do have some answers to your questions regarding the PNP registry book(s).

When outsiders arrive in Yaviza (or El Real), they are required to sign in and inform the Panamanian National Police of intent to ascend the Rio Tuira.

We did not do this. Instead, we decided to skip this formality. In El Real, we met a Colombian, a black, who said that he could guide us into Colombia himself. At first, he said that he needed to return to his hometown in Cordoba, then later he said that he didn't need to return to Colombia, but he needed the money. He said that his name was Lino Barco and that he lived in the village of Capeti (later he told the PNP he lived in Yape). It was a shaky start to our relationship, but we carried him with us to Boca de Cupe. He attempted to cheat us a half dozen times (marked-up prices on chartering piraguas from the Kuna, changing his daily guide rate, and finally he tried to get us to pay twice the normal rental rate for a shack we let in Boca de Cupe from an acquaintance of his. We were not easy targets, though, and he got nothing.) In less than 24 hours we realized that Lino wasn't the man for the job, and, much to his angry dismay, we sent him on his way, back downriver to Capeti or Yape.

Prior to this, though, while still en route to Boca de Cupe by piragua canoe, we were required to stop at 3 military stations set up on the banks of the Tuira. These PNP cuarteles, as they're called, were established to record traffic on the river. 24 hours a day, the stations are manned with American M-16's at the ready. Each stop requires the passengers of the piragua to disembark and show papers that are then recorded in a registry log. The PNP soldiers have walkie-talkies that can reach to the next station.

When we arrived at the first stop in Vista Alegre, the commanding officer radioed El Real to see why he was not notified of our arrival. As a result of our failure to register in El Real, we were held up for 45 minutes while they decided whether or not to send us back downriver to start over, properly. The Colombian guide, Lino, made the PNP very uneasy. As politically incorrect as it may be, the Colombians have endured desperate conditions and become desperate people. The soldiers treated Lino like he was a Wild Card, someone who, while behaving at the moment, could in the next instant go berserk and kill their entire platoon. It is very tense in Darien.

In the end, through respect and an impassioned speech about my lifelong dream to see a Harpy eagle in the wild, I persuaded them to let us continue upriver. They recorded our info and Lino's info, and radioed ahead to the cuartel in Union Choco, where the process was repeated and they radioed to the final PNP outpost in Panama, which is, of course, Boca de Cupe. In Boca de Cupe, we proceeded to the PNP station at the rear of the town where our passports were confiscated and held over-night while they decided whether or not they would let us proceed (they don't really have a choice, but when it came to holding our passports overnight, I chose to pick my battles – my travel partner was a little frantic, but it was the right call.)

In the morning, passports were returned, more dire warnings were issued – and the promise that if anything happened beyond Boca de Cupe, we were on our own; nobody goes even into Pucuro with the blessing of the Panamanian government. Effectively, the not-so-long arm of Panama law reaches only to Boca de Cupe.

All guides and outsiders and Indians must sign in at each cuartel on the river. Furthermore, there is a displaced Colombian exile population of Blacks residing with marginal legality in Boca de Cupe and Yape. They all seem to know each other very well.

Has anybody gone to Boca de Cupe with photos of Paul and Tom? There would have to be answers. The rainforest is vast, but the human population is small and concentrated in tiny pockets. There are people in Boca de Cupe who must know exactly who went into the jungle with your son and his pal. I believe that the unsolicited counsel I extended in my last letter was premature. There are many details that could easily be checked before the reverse trip to Payita could be required.

In reference to checking, I thought it odd that I would not have heard anything about this disappearance before receiving your e-mail. I try to keep my ear close to the ground when it comes to all things Central American. I searched the archives of The *Times* in London and the *Irish Times* and found not even a mention. Why is that?

I did find that a Kieran (K.K.) Winder, with some sort of association with the *Irish Times*, has made attempts to find Paul (findpaul@ireland.com). I found no mention of the Hart Dyke's missing son – and only a confirmation that the family is registered as residents of a stately home. I learned that Paul is 29-years of age, over 6-feet tall, and fair headed.

Why has a bigger deal not been made of this disappearance? Has there been a conscious effort to keep this from creating international pressure on Colombia and Panama? Is there some plan to keep this below the radars of the two governments so that search efforts can be effected without any monitoring by them?

I know that we Americans have a lousy reputation for being brash and too bold. It is well-deserved. Sometimes it is also well-served. What can I do to help you? The offer is not so altruistic as it sounds. I would like, one night in the not-so-distant future, to be able to sleep again. Do you have maps of the area? Can you place in your mind the areas that I describe?

Coincidentally... I received an e-mail from Albert of the Eco-Village Training Center. He said that he was forwarded my last note to you. I have no problem with you doing that, however, I will not honour his request for the GPS coordinates through Darien. He is cocky enough to die quickly, and his line, 'Your letter was highly informative and prompts me to check the insurance on my expensive cameras, laptop, and other gear. Beyond that, I will leave to fate,' leads me to wonder what he thinks about checking the edge on his machete, or the dryness of his powder. He wrote that he intends to go only to a village near Unguia, but 'The coordinates you have taken could be useful to me, although I do not intend to travel to Pucuro.' As such, I will not respond to his request, knowing that a pocketful of coordinates can do nothing but lure him into a false sense of security. He can play Jungle Boy in Costa Rica. The Kuna don't need him –

and, if he's not looking for Paul and Tom, he doesn't need to be in Darien.

P.S. – Obviously, you don't owe me any explanations for anything I've questioned. Quite the contrary, I feel that I owe you, and your wife. If communicating with me becomes too much of a distraction, or too disquieting, I realize that I must understand and accept that. Please do not feel the need to jeopardize your search efforts in order to keep me informed. This is not to be about my feelings of guilt – it is to be about finding Paul or finding answers.

July 14

I replied to James Spring: "Do not worry, I have a firm stomach for disquiet. Discussion will not disquiet me; all knowledge is useful. It's facts that do disquiet... and they are facts and cannot be changed.

Your description of the police checks was very helpful. I have passed it on to the British Embassy in Panama, and told them that they must make it plain to the Colombian police that we know that the police must know the names of the two 'guides'. I asked the British Embassy to get the names of the 'guides' from the police two weeks ago, but there has only been silence since then. Unfortunately, the British Embassy has very few local contacts and very little local knowledge. They are just plodding civil servants.

As for publicity in the UK, I sent articles to the *Daily Telegraph*, the *Times* and the *Guardian* correspondent in Colombia and the first two didn't even reply. The *Daily Mail* (a right-wing rag, read avidly by women) was interested , but about 3 days ago I told them to delay it for at least a week, because Sarah Hart Dyke didn't want publicity at the same time as her initiative. I also am in contact with a few journalists, whom I might use when the Hart Dyke initiative peters out. Then I will probably get them to aim at the *Times*, or *Daily Telegraph* (each demands exclusiveness, and it would be a pity for that exclusiveness to be a rag rather than a world-known paper).

The holes in your knowledge is due to you coming late on the scene."

So, I described what I had been able to find out in Panama. Then I went on.

"From the above, the likelihood, I think, is about equal: the shifty Colombian guides might have done the lads in after they had got a safe distance away from the village – just for the dollars in their pockets; or the Indians of Paya might have taken offence at the cultural ineptitudes and the fact that they did not use them as guides (and the heaped up incidents of the last few years – Pat Upton's, the burning of other villages, etc. Lips would, of course, remain sealed.

Your other findings on the internet were valid – enthusiastic nephews in Ireland set up the FINDPAUL site , and it and an advert in a Bogota paper did get quite a few responses – but all from goodwilled city people (mainly in Bogota) who hadn't real knowledge about the Darien. I still correspond with an Eddy O'Brien in Bogota. He cannot believe that the lads could have been killed (and I lap up the comfort) because everywhere else in Colombia, except the Darien, they would have been held for ransom.

As for the tardiness of my searches, it was perhaps helped by Paul 'disappearing' for about 2 months in the Sahara 6 years ago, so we were slow to move. He didn't keep us too well informed. Glad you discouraged Albert, I hadn't noticed his name on the eco-village memos.

I am at the moment waiting to find out more about the Sarah Hart Dyke initiative: it looks like a standard detective agency without enough local contacts. She is flying to Bogota next week for 3 weeks. I am trying to make sure that no sensitive names can possibly be given to the Colombian army.

If I decide to take a parallel initiative, it would be just to go to the eco-village near Unguia, and with that as cover contact the two traders you mentioned, and get talking to them. Thus, relying on them, with possible promises of future reward… Would you be willing to accompany with all expenses paid for you? Your face would assure them. But note that I am not proposing going along the path (certainly beyond Arguia), or carrying guns or anything, or even having to be secret about going into Unguia because of using the eco-cover. I'd have to get the agreement of the eco-village people, and have assurances that the two traders would be located and waiting for me. It's not a definite plan yet. Just a possibility."

12 Let's Try the Newspapers

July 5

My nephew Stephen was very keen on a newspaper article. Remember he said he had somehow put an advert in a newspaper *El Tiempo* in Bogota… and got a response.

Herman from the hostel in Bogota also recommended it, arguing: it might raise the profile of the incident and might draw someone out of the woodwork who knows the area. It might even persuade the Panamanian police to stop stone-walling.

But how does one get an article into the press in the UK, and which paper to try first?

I did submit a very short article to the *Daily Mail* at the start of June, but the woman on the Foreign Desk that I spoke to seemed grumpy and uninterested. She totally ignored the e-mail that I sent her.

So, I tried again. I had written an article of about 200 words, and offered it to the *Times*, the *Daily Mail* and the *Telegraph*. The *Guardian* has instructed me to go through their foreign correspondent in Colombia. The article is fairly bland starting with the sentence "Two British backpackers have been missing in the Darien jungle area between Panama and Colombia for nearly 4 months and are feared dead".

But in case some editor wanted the article to be 300 words, say, I added two appendices covering the following: memos each way between Paul and Tom arranging the trip, a catch up of what happened, breaking into Paul's Hotmail and finding out who Paul's companion was, James Spring's description of his traverse of the Darien Gap, and my sending the Indian up the trail in search of information.
These two appendices together add up to 300 words, and the idea was that the editor could extract bits from one or other of them to increase the article to whatever he wants.

July 9

The *Daily Mail* now indicated that they were quite keen on my article. I've had to ask them to delay it because the

Hart Dykes now don't want any publicity at all. Basically, they think that an article will harm the investigation. We think that an article may help the investigation, especially with the stonewalling Panamanian police.

To please the Hart Dykes, I tried to get the *Telegraph* to halt publication also, emailing them two or three times and phoning them twice.

July 14

Nine days after sending the initial article Anne Barraclough on the *Times* newspaper got wind of the story and phoned me up. I referred her to the pieces that I had sent to them over 10 days ago, which they had ignored. So they suddenly thought it was quite a gripping story, and they wanted to make it into a full-page feature. They wanted to send a photographer the next day to our home... which they did.

July 16

The *Sunday Telegraph* had today broken the story with a full-page article about the orchid hunters, Tom Hart Dyke and Paul Winder. The fact was that Paul has no interest in orchids, and Tom didn't do this particular Darien Gap trip for the sake of orchids: it was simply an adventure.

It was true that a horticultural organisation had sponsored Tom in his travels, and it was perhaps them who who gave some of the information to the papers.

Either way the Hart Dykes were quite annoyed because they wanted no publicity whatsoever. And they had their reasons.

July 19, Wednesday

However, the *Times* came in quick succession with a two-page article in Wednesday's overseas news section.

I will not bore the reader of this book with the major text of the article because it mainly consisted of what this book so far has described, put in a slightly different way.

But it then introduced the topic of the chances of the two coming out of the jungle alive and recorded me as saying that I thought they were slim.

And adding, "The distressing thing is that if Paul is dead, we will never know where he died and how." And there is the question that won't go away. "Why, why did you have to go into extreme danger?" Even though we know the answer: "It would be a good story when we got back, and a satisfaction, and I thought my luck would hold out."

Such was the article in the *Times*.

July 20

From 8 am in the morning after the *Times* article, we were besieged by the press. The phone had been going so much that we had to set it on the answerphone. It seemed the other papers had also found the article and are on the trail. It was good that I had taken the day off work.

We let the *Times* and the BBC TV ITV crews in. They did a preliminary interview before they started the cameras rolling. But when that happened, they asked me a question which we had not rehearsed. They asked, "How do you feel?" And in saying the words, "You do not expect your children to die?" I broke down. I asked them not to show that bit, but that's the only bit they showed. They ignored my 10 minutes waffle about what actually happened.

When the *Times* photographer came, I kept asking him why he wanted to photograph me, when Anne was more photogenic.

July 21

Some of the local Chelmsford papers jazzed the story up – perhaps because we had the phone on answerphone, and they could not get valid material. In one of their articles Paul is an Indiana Jones, and a botanist. Another paper attributed to me far more faith in Paul's return than I in fact have. That paper did interview me and tried to get me to say that there was a 95% chance of Paul returning; in fact I thought it was far less, so I asked him to compromise and say that there was a "reasonable chance" of his returning. "Reasonable" can mean different things to different people.

Having learned from the incident of the *Sunday Telegraph* how good journalists can be as detectives, I thought it might be best if we knocked some of the memos off the FIND-PAUL site or restricted access to it. For example, I would like to keep the memos about an eco-village and names such as those of James Spring and Margarito, the Indian, away from the media. So, I asked Stephen Winder to do this.

The phone calls kept coming in from other TV stations and film feature makers.

I was told that the story had broken in the Panamanian

and Colombian papers also, but no response from any contacts there.

July 22

I had an appeal from a woman, asking me to discourage her son from going into the Darien Gap. She said, "He seems drawn to dangerous places." So, I sent an e-mail to the lad basically describing the danger
and how you can be killed for the crimes of others, and asking him if he can speak Spanish like a native.

Predictably I got no reply... but I think the lad gave up the idea.
13 A Promise of Information or... a Con?

The article in the *Times* was published on Wednesday July 19th.

Let's summarise how we felt then.
We had come to a dead-end on all fronts in our search. Paul's contacts knew nothing of what had happened to him since March 7th. We had learned especially that official channels were no use, despite their willingness... We suspected that the Panamanian Police were deliberately withholding information, since they had access to the books kept at the staging posts on the river Tuira, and yet did not come back with any comments on records of the lads. Though the staff at the British Embassies were always willing to listen, they simply did not have local contacts or adequate resources for this kind of operation.

July 23

On Sunday after the publication of the article in the *Times* a FAX came through our machine with a strange handwritten message from a person who signed himself Mike. The sender phoned up shortly afterwards saying that his name was Mike Hills, and that he lived in Holland.

The FAX said: "Maybe I can help with the disappearance of your son. I have some very useful contacts. In Panama I have some 7-8 of these contacts that are unofficial, and want to stay that way. I have used them before with the location of missing persons, even after they were missing a few months. I still think that if there is a chance it should be taken.

I shall have to meet you in the very near future."

He then phoned us, basically saying the same thing.

Myself and my wife, Anne, scratched our heads at this strange FAX message.

We both agreed that this Mike seemed dodgy, and from his language and accent uneducated, but if he had these contacts, then he was more likely to succeed than any official route.

A private individual operating through contacts is what is needed, and this Mike could be the thing. We are not certain, but we could try for a while.

July 24

We phoned Mike Hills in Holland, and queried him about his background. He said that he traded in guns as his main occupation, and in the Darien Gap area he traded them both to FARC, the guerrilla group, and to the paramilitaries. I queried about the paramilitaries, because I had heard that the USA rather supplied the paramilitaries with guns.

He suggested that I come over to meet him at Ostend in

Belgium towards the end of the week if I wanted to proceed further.

With a view to this meeting he FAXed a photograph of himself, and asked me to send a photo of myself to him for identification purposes.

I was not alert enough at this stage to record the landlines FAX number.

14
AN EXTRAORDINARY PROPOSAL
& ITS UNWINDING

July 14

James Spring came up with this extraordinary offer: "I apologize for taking so much time to respond. I had much to think about. And people to inform, explanations to provide.

I will return to the Darien. I am not a wealthy man, but I can help with some of my expenses. And I, of course, have all of the gear necessary. The last Darien trek put me back substantially. I seek no recompense for my efforts or time. My reward will be putting closure on this tragic event, and knowing that I did all that I could to serve the families of two missing boys that were encouraged by tales of our survival.

I am not a soldier-of-fortune. I am not a survivalist. I went into the Darien with the belief that I wanted to see remote Kuna cultures living as they've lived for centuries. I know that this was a lie. I went in to see if I could come out the other side. I went in for the wrong reasons.

I have done many things in my life for the wrong reasons. My "vacation" destinations look like headline news. El Salvador. Nicaragua. Guatemala. Chiapas. Belfast.

Yes, even Belfast, where, as you know, there is much ado about nothing. Perhaps the most brilliant insight I've garnered came from a cab driver who was a Loyalist in Belfast.

He said to me, "I am a Loyalist. But I realize that if I had been born two streets over, I would have been a Nationalist. And I would have been fighting against what I am today."

I wish that I had let the words sink in before I travelled to Darien. I knew that there was a war. Like all wars, it is senseless for either side to be involved. It was even more senseless for me to be involved. Paul wasn't lost in the Sahara. He was lost within himself. I understand this. It is easy for the world to call him stupid. It would be easy for me to say the same had I not been Paul once. Whatever it was that distanced him from society, he sought to compensate for it in his travels. And when he returned, he called out, 'Look. I have survived. I am alive. Doesn't that give me merit? Aren't I worthy?'

Surviving the Gap made me see the holes in this logic. I vowed to stop seeking these senseless thrills. I am 32-years-old, I suppose you didn't know that. It is time for me to make my place in a society that has not previously been so inviting. It is time for the chip to fall from my shoulder. These are concepts I have long grappled with. I have lived by the teachings of Nietzsche. The errant philosophies of Ayn Rand. The glorified inspirations of Hemingway. And the path delivered me to what is, doubtless to a practical man such as yourself, an obvious doorstep.

There is no such thing as an intrepid jungle explorer. We are men who run from the things that terrify us or reject us. Respect. Love. Intimacy. These are beasts that we are ill-suited to face. So we escape beneath the relative comforts of the jungle canopy.

Regardless, when I received your first e-mail, I knew that

it might lead to an invitation back into Colombia. I returned to the physical training schedule I had implemented prior to our trek in January. I am in near top condition. I've been assembling gear, filling voids in my inventory. For the first time in my life, I am now running toward the challenge. I believe that there is no more valid reason to go to Darien than searching for answers to your son's disappearance. I feel largely safe and comforted by the knowledge of the area that I picked up during my first trek through. And I realize that I am not only going to Darien to find two missing British boys, I am returning to bury the boy that I once was.

I spoke to my employer and let him know that I might need to leave for a couple of weeks. Needless to say, I had already used up all of my vacation time. But I feel certain that my job will be held for me.

So, on to details... I have been keeping ranked lists of various concerns. What could have happened to the boys? Where could they be? What more do I need to know? What more do I need (supplies)? What must I do before I depart? What is the best plan of attack? I have many pages written with an evolving list of answers to all of these questions. In my mind, these are the objectives:

1) Find where the trail ends, whether it be clues on a jungle floor, or British-made steel in a Kuna hovel, or the discovery of the names of the parties responsible.
2) Find the names of the guides who led Paul and Tom into the Gap.
3) Provide names of likely suspects to your embassy and the Colombian government (through some of the new doors opened by Colombia's President Pastrana).

American interest in this case will help, as our government just extended $1.3 billion to their efforts to curb the production of narcotics. It will help if the international community pushes for the guilty parties to be brought to justice, if justice is not first effected on the jungle floor. I believe that these are the answers that you seek. I know that they represent my own.

From your last e-mail, I fear that there are a couple of grave miscalculations on the board right now. I need to know what the Hart Dyke family is doing. Their actions could inadvertently put our efforts, and lives, in danger. Has a reward been offered? If so, to whom? The promise of a reward in a place like Colombia may not bode well for us, either. If I get too close, somebody may decide that there is only one way to stop a 'bounty hunter' from snooping. They also might realize that if Paul and Tom are worth something dead, I might be, too.

What is the story with Eco-Village? Did Paul have any contact with them? Why do you believe they can be of service to you? Just because your neighbour lives next door to your car doesn't mean he can fix the transmission. Their village of Sasardi appears so irrelevant to me that I wonder why you feel compelled to visit. It is not on the path out of the Gap. We did not see it in our travels.

Furthermore, there is no way in the world that the two merchants, Albero and Eliseo, will go there. There is an even less chance that they will stay there to be met by you. And, if they share any guilt, they will disappear into the jungle. If the Eco-Village did get involved in the business of trying to hold people, they can all kiss their lives away, too. I visited their website. Their concept of peaceful co-existence with nature, as exemplified by aboriginal cultures, is admirable, if not completely idiotic when established near Colombia's Cordoba province.

You wrote that you wouldn't want to pass Unguia secretly because of using the Eco-Village cover. The best cover is stealth. I am certain that you have read the accounts of the three Americans who were killed by FARC rebels five months prior to our trek. They were in Colombia visiting Indian villages under the auspices of the Native American People's Coalition. They were murdered and their bodies burned.

Please don't assume that I am trying to play James Bond here. People really do die. The law is useless. People are duplicitous. Machetes are sharp. Guns are powerful. The jungle is harsh. I am not trying to do anything but find answers and survive.

Are there good photos of the boys in existence? Do you have many copies? I need a list of gear that they carried. Brands and colours of backpacks, ponchos, hats, knives, machetes, clothes, toilet paper, food wrappers, energy bars, drink packets, oral rehydration salt envelopes, cooking stove, stove fuel, guidebooks, pens, matches, lighters, batteries, flashlights, medical supplies, currency, film, cameras, water purifiers, utensils, pots, pans, dishes, tea bags, bug repellent, sheets, blankets, fishing supplies, etc. Remember, anything of any jungle value is being used by somebody right at this moment.

It is the peak of the rainy season – the worst time to travel. Footprints are washed away. Many clues may have been washed into bushes or downriver. What did the postcard from Yaviza say? What final contacts did Tom have with his family or friends?

Coincidentally, if the Chief in Paya truly had concerns about the Colombian guides, they were probably not Albero and Eliseo, though it is not safe to make assumptions.

My biggest concern right now, though, is your presence. I have not seen you, obviously, so this cannot be a judgement to cause you offence. I worry about your physical condition. I worry about the options of fight or flight, and how you might do in either situation. I still hear a loud sense of civility in your plan to enter a hostile, hostile land. Twice during our trek we brandished machetes, prepared to fight. Are you up for that? If not, you risk both of our lives.

You say that you have only a desire to go to Arquia. Both Unguia and Arquia are in the middle of the paramilitary's hot zones. I can't outgun paramilitary, I must be prepared to run. Are you up for that? If not, I'm obviously not leaving you alone in the jungle, which means that both of our lives are, again, at risk. I have an idea. You won't like it, but I feel it's best.

We meet in Panama City? We can fly together on a small plane from Panama City to El Real. From El Real we can take a piragua canoe upriver to the PNP cuarteles at Vista Alegre, Union Choco, and Boca de Cupe. We will find the names of the Colombians who registered simultaneously with your son. There is the chance that we will find nothing. But in Boca de Cupe we will get answers from villagers. There is a man, whose wife keeps tabs on everybody passing through. She knew that we were going to arrive a day before we knocked on her door. She had already found out about our 'guide' Lino Barco and voiced her concerns.

I may need to continue on to Pucuro in order to get information from the Colombian-Kuna woman Linda who I described in an earlier e-mail. She may be able to tell me about the guides and the mystery 'armed men'. After we get our info, we head back downriver to El Real and take a plane either back to Panama City or arrange a charter to Apartado in Colombia. You travel with me one hour by taxi to Turbo where I will take a boat to Unguia, hike eight hours to Arquia, and find out if Paul ever arrived. I'll also find out where Albero and Eliseo are. If it is known that the Colombian Army has their names, they will dive so deep into the jungle that they will not be seen for months. Or longer. It is better to go in as swiftly and silently as possible.

The jungle telegraph that Patricia Upton alludes to in her book is very real. I am certain that everybody knows that the two boys have disappeared. The culprits are on heightened alert. They, too, will have the option of fight or flight. I'd rather not have you there for this moment. It is not worth the risk.

If the boys made it to Arquia, they were probably taken by paramilitary. The pursuit of actual culprits in Unguia will be tough. If the boys' trail ends in Payita, it will be more important that we know the names of the guides.

I know that much of this has turned to rambling. I apologize. There are many factors and facets to consider.

The only other request that I have is for the use of an Iridium (or comparable) satellite telephone. I would like to have the ability to call you in Apartado with results from the jungle. I would also like to have the ability to let people know where I am so that we can avoid the unlikely need for sending somebody searching the entire Darien Gap for my whereabouts. I believe that Iridium phones are priced at approximately $500, with airtime charges of $4 per minute.

Please feel free to call me, or write me with any of the info I've requested. I would hope that if you decide to accept my offer of assistance that we do not delay its implementation. I can be ready in 48 hours. I can also arrange all air transportation. I promise to respond more promptly and succinctly to your reply. Thank you for offering to allow me to be a part of the resolution."

July 15

I sent a stalling reply: "This is just a stalling memo. I got your memo and its extraordinary offer.
But remember I too have a conscience.
Will reply when I've absorbed it all."

And followed it with another stalling memo: "I call this a Holding memo, because I still have to take in the implications of your suggestions… and this is not a commitment…
All of your philosophical thoughts at the start are valid, but I will reply on them later, separately as they deserve. They and the rest of your memo is not at all rambling.
And, by the way, with me you can never give offence, or fear to tell the truth.
I live in Chelmsford, Essex, 30 miles east of London.
I would expect you to bear no expenses, and I must at least cover accommodation expenses (mortgage or whatever) in San Diego, for the time you are away from work. And I would need to be certain that your job was held for you.
Now a few agreements and qualifications.

Agreements & assurances:

1) I agree about the eco village. They are taking a long time to reply, and they are obviously afraid of their neutrality to politics being compromised. They would have been a useful intermediary when I was thinking of going in myself, merely to ask questions, and I thought it would be a safe haven. I am e-mailing them now to say that they should do nothing and forget the whole affair: I had asked the American contact to ask the Spanish speaking fellow in the eco-village to put out feelers for Felipe in Archya and possibly ask him if he knew where the two traders were just now , but since they did not reply, I assume that the message was not passed on to the eco village itself until the political implications of involvement were approved at 'Head Office'.

2) No reward has been offered, so that's safe.

3) The Hart Dykes have raked up a standard Detective Agency in Bogota, who will find out nothing and disturb no stones. The detective agency will bring Sarah Hart Dyke from the airport to her hotel, accompany her to meet the British Ambassador, accompany her to meet the head of the Red Cross – all saying sweet words and finding out nothing, and charging $600 per day (plus expenses). We have made it plain that we are not contributing.

4) I am not physically fit in your sense of the word. I'd have no problem with a 3000 ft mountain, and I'm slim, but to run for it with a pack on my back, I'm afraid I'd be caught up with easily. The weather is still quite cool here this summer, and acclimatizing to the heat would contribute to problems.

5) No Western sense of justice will confuse the issue.

Qualifications:

1) No problem with photos but... I will not be able to give many details of his gear. Paul had been nearly 5 months away from home by that stage, and his postcards or e-mails were brief and sought to be jolly (or bravura-ish), rather than to give information. I'll do some research on Paul's rucksack and camera – but the killers or captors would have taken those probably.

2) As for mobile phones, I went into many mobile phone shops here and they checked their suppliers international lists and said that none claimed to operate in Panama. But if you think that it might be difficult to get an Iridium one in Apartado, then make some enquiries in San Diego.

3) Of course, it is not 100% certain that the lads followed your route. If the Paya Indians had been responsible for the murder, and if the chief of Paya was devious enough, he could have given false information to the Indian I had sent up.
Is there any question I haven't answered?
And what area of San Diego are you in – N/S/E/W – for money transfer.

There is no rational objective in hurrying.
So the thoughts are for later in the week... but not definite yet, remember.

My wife also likes to delay every decision a bit (it normally turns out to be wise). She's a bit confused just today because the story has broken in the UK press today (and we have the answer-phone on at the moment, to keep away the papers and the television stations till we have thought things out and are ready for them).

Anyway, that's some thoughts to keep you going."

July 16

James has sent another e-mail.

"I'm sorry that this e-mail is arriving so much later than I said it would. I have been studying and training so hard. Not a moment has passed that has not been consumed with the thoughts of preparations for this trek.

Writing these e-mails, while absolutely imperative, take a good deal out of me. The added bonus in composing them, however, is that it creates an opportunity for me to lay out plans and double check their logic.

The answers to the questions that you submitted are valuable. A couple of key points were missed, or perhaps brushed off too easily.

And as for identifying any gear they might have had any info will help. It sounds like Tom was not much of a traveller. All of his gear will be brand new. Where did he buy it? What does it look like? Did he have better communications with his family? Do the Hart Dykes know anything about this gear, food? Did they carry wallets? What did they look like? What did Tom's final communications say?

Speaking of Tom, I would like to have the opportunity to e-mail Sarah Hart Dyke. Up until this point I have not felt the compulsion to communicate with her. Now, though, I'm realizing that it is the 11th hour, and any tiny little titbit of info she might offer could be essential to our success.

I am printing up photos of Albero and Eliseo. I took clear face shots of each. I will be searching for them also. Another detail that I forgot to mention. Albero and Eliseo told me that they planned to leave Arquia and move to Pucuro. They said that the dangers of living in Colombia had escalated to a mortal degree.

Both men received tentative permission from Chief Gabriel. I witnessed this while I was in their presence. Albero and Eliseo said that Pucuro was a good option because the women were so beautiful (and, oddly enough, they are).

Please e-mail me the photos that you plan to reprint of Paul and Tom. I would like to make sure that they fit with my idea of what is a clear, identifiable photo.

I am considering creating photo flyers in Spanish that could be left with chiefs in my wake. I am undecided at this point.

I have a person set up here in San Diego to receive regular communications from me. He will record the dates, times, and GPS coordinates of my position so that if anything happens, all will know where my trail ends.

Let's talk to Margarito in Panama. We can book an Aeroperlas flight to Darien while in Panama City.

My cell phone is available to you 24 hours a day. Call me with any questions. Sometimes our e-mail checking is out of synch and causes unnecessary delays.

Turns out Paul first contacted her in November, with the idea of Unguia already in mind. Our success only confirmed his suspicions – that the path to Unguia was the best option.

I have delegated many of my tasks to capable people this week. A friend of mine has found a satnav that will work in the Darien region. The unit weighs 5 pounds, 3 ounces. Rental cost is $250 for the first week and $22/day thereafter. Additional batteries, of which I assume I'll want three are available at just $5 each. They have a website at www.out-fitterelectronics.com. I've not yet checked it out.

I have not used your credit card to order anything to this point. I'll make a tentative reservation for a Friday departure (the Aeroperlas flight leaves Panama City for Darien/El Real on Saturday at 8:30 am). I'll keep the return date open and call them back with your credit card info after you have confirmed or adjusted my plan.

I am actually somewhat relieved to hear confirmations of Paul's cavalier attitude. Whatever happened, I feel certain that we can do better by respecting the culture with requisite humility and conviction. Answers will come our way.

Please let me know at your soonest convenience.
James."

July 16

A MAJOR BOMBSHELL!

James' friend and brother have got onto me and said that they had sussed out what James had intended to do, and that they were very worried by it. Also, that it would be a particular worry to James' parents and girlfriend.

Also, Anne was very worried about the possible dangers, and said we must stop it.

Obviously, my stalling memos had not been taken seriously enough, and by answering his questions I had obviously lead him on also.

So, I wrote an e-mail.

"Dear James,
Hold, halt, stop.
I called some of my previous memos 'holding' memos, because, although my mind kept thinking of details and answering your questions, I also said I had not agreed to the basic question: 'Could I let you go in and risk your life?' I too may have got carried away.

Also, I think you are getting tense.

You yourself so deeply described your past in perspective. There is a danger of the present going out of perspective.

My wife cannot bear the thought of you going missing. We would have that on our conscience. I am quite confident that there are people who would miss you, though you do not wear your heart on your sleeve.

What I originally proposed was a limited exercise – basically of asking question in the relative safety of Archya on the other side. It has escalated into something that may be too dangerous.

So let's stop for a while. I suggest you stop training, and take a rest from memo writing, and we calm down.

I'll refund any expenses whether we take this up again or not.

I greatly appreciate you, and I think you are extremely generous, and it is wonderful to deal with you… but let's have a few days' calm."

July 17

James replied: "I appreciate your concerns, and will, of course, stop all but the physical training. What danger is there in me having a heightened level of fitness?

There is nothing to reimburse. The few things that I have ordered represent needs that I essentially had, anyway.

Any steps that I have taken are ones that could be stopped at any point.

When you wrote that we might consider leaving at the end of the week, I figured it was better to get prepared now, and have the option of leaving at week's end, rather than have the week end with no preparations in place. I can stop anything at any point.

I understand that you want to think things through as thoroughly as possible. I've been doing the same (hence no concrete plans). If this trip is to happen, though, I would like it to be as soon as possible. I figure I'll be gone for about two weeks. My brother is getting married August 15th. I would like to attend.

I am prepared to do limited checking in Arquia. Answers may come quickly and easily. I might be home in 7 days. If not, I feel it best to be prepared for every conceivable outcome, and perhaps a few not yet conceived.

The thing that keeps me from sleeping well has already occurred. There is nothing we can do to stop it at this point. Your son, inspired by our success, followed our trail toward Colombia. He is somewhere in between. I am the most qualified human being in the world to find him. That is not a boast, it is a horrible reality. I wish that I had never heard of the Darien.

But, everyday, for the rest of my life, I will fret over the dishonour of not answering the call that I was given. I will worry about the tiniest possibility that I could have effected Paul's extraction – or even helped bring culprits towards justice.

If you worry about my physical death, I ask you to consider my soul. A little bit of me will die every day for the rest of my life.

Our lives are entwined at this point, yours and mine. That idiot Hemingway wrote that parents should not outlive their children. I guess, like you, I believe he is right. Let's dispatch with our pain and wondering.

I want the killings in Colombia to stop. In the absence of that, I want people to stop going to Colombia. Anything that I can do to realize these aims will help deliver me.

I am not, in the least, a New Age thinker. But I can't help but think that when a father, through an ethereal medium such as this, 10,000 miles away, finds me, who is sadly the best candidate for the job, and wants help finding answers to his son's disappearance – I have a spiritual duty. This has never happened before. This will never happen again. How do I shirk this and live for the rest of my life?

From this point forward, I'll do as little or as much as you see fit. I feel that there is a certain level of expediency required at this point. At least, I'd like to think that there is a slight chance that expediency is required. In pursuing that, I ask only that you help me honour the scant other obligations in my life by helping me to get back to my home as quickly as possible.

Please advise. At your leisure. After a good night's sleep.

And tell Mrs. Winder that your requests have not caused me grief. They have given me the grandest opportunity to challenge my character, and the rewards for that are priceless and eternal. Good night."

July 22

James' brother and two friends guessed what James was planning to do, and they somehow got my email address and wrote to me, encouraging me to stop James in his tracks.

At the same time, they felt that they were going behind James' back and being disloyal, but they saw it as the only way out.

I, of course, immediately emailed James, saying that I had to forbid him positively from going into the Darien again, and I admitted that by answering his many questions, I had inadvertently encouraged him in his wild enterprise. Mea culpa.

So, having vetted their decision with me, they ambushed James at breakfast this morning and brought everything out into the open. He tried to parry this by saying that he would stay within Panama and not go into Colombia.

He recounted that at that point his girlfriend grabbed him by the arm and said: "You don't get it. People love you. They want to keep you alive. Do you not see it?"

James said: "At that point I saw that even though the risks of going to Paya were less, they weren't any less ludicrous."

He wrote to me afterwards saying how difficult the last fortnight had been for him and how he recognised now that he had been trying to be the hero with no certain benefit coming from it. How few of us would be humble enough to admit that!

15
A MEETING AT OSTEND

July 20

Mike Hills had not mentioned money at first, but we expected him to.

Now he says that he needs $7,500 in cash since he would have to bribe various people, especially a corrupt Panamian policeman.

He wants me to hand over this money in Ostend tomorrow.

I was at work, so I phoned Anne and asked her to draw out $5000 from the bank. She very kindly did that.

I said to Mike on the phone that I had no proof of his abilities or qualifications in this case, and that I was only willing to pay $5,000 over and that on the condition of "success": i.e. that all money would be paid back unless the following conditions were met: "If the lads are dead, then we must be given the exact location of their bodies, and that if they are being held captive then we must be given the means of contacting their captors". He readily agreed to this condition.

To make certain, I wrote this condition underneath the photograph of myself that I faxed over to help us to recognise each other tomorrow. I also mentioned that this was a large amount of money for us, and that we had difficulty in raising it.

Strange this Mike: he seems a shady character, yet he

uses his real name, sends us his photograph, and is confident enough of success to make this agreement which no detective agency would make.

July 21

I set off to Dover for the crossing to Ostend next day.

Anne was quite worried about my going off, but I knew that there was no danger since I had arranged to meet this Mike Hills in a public place – the café in the Ferry port.

After a quarter of an hour wandering through and around the café, I recognised him. We got down to business.

First, he gave me a photocopy of his UK passport. He wrote down his address in Breskens. He showed me electricity and other bills with this address and his name on them. He also gave me some correspondence about his Social Security number in Holland, seemingly addressed to him. That openness seemed to support his honest intent.

I again asked him how he knew about the case, and he again said that the Panamanian policeman had contacted him, and he found out more by asking a journalist friend who worked for Der Spiegel to search the internet for any details, and from that he had got our names and location. He denied all knowledge of it being in the UK papers.

The crooked policeman had also said someone was holding Traveller's Chequesfrom the lads, and Mike had phoned the American Express office in the UK about them, but they had not got back to him yet.

He repeated that his crooked policeman had said he had definite information on the lads.

I asked him to draw a map of the Darien, and he could not do so: but I relented on pressing him because he said that the expert on that area was Pedro, not himself.

I also queried him again on the language: how did he speak to anyone in the Darien since he admitted that he did not speak Spanish. He said that his common-law wife spoke Spanish, and she did the communicating. Also that he relied on his "man", Pedro, who was in Holland at the moment.

He presented me with a FAX which he said had come from his contact as an invoice for the information – but this time the amount was for $25,000 in all, but he said that $7,500 was all that was needed as an advance. He said he beat them down. I queried the fact that this contact had a FAX machine in the Darien jungle. The FAX (which looked quite fishy, since it talked about the "goods to be delivered") also said "Payment to be in Advance". But it was in English: strange, they only speak Spanish there.

He said he was in a hurry to send Pedro out there on his gun-running operation, and that Mike himself was going to Russia for 3 weeks to pick up cheap guns. When I queried him a little later in the conversation as to how we would keep in contact since he would be off in Russia, he said that his mobile phone would keep him in contact. Besides, he changed his story to saying that he was only going back and forward to Russia.

I repeated again that we were only willing to give money on the criteria of "success", i.e. all money would be paid back unless, "If the lads were found to be dead, then the exact location of their bodies or equipment, if held captive then the means of contacting their captors." He again agreed to this.

He said that one reason why he was interested in helping me was because his daughter had disappeared in the East some years ago, but that later she was found.

By this stage it was obvious that some of the things he said didn't seem to hold water, but others seemed plausible.

I decided to take the risk all other avenues seemed closed.

I gave him $5,000. I also gave him photographs of the lads, dental records etc.

He asked for as much information as possible about contacts in the area, and I said I would FAX him the basic facts of the story and the names of gossips and others in the villages. I even e-mailed him a map of the area. I wonder, was that a mistake?

I caught the afternoon boat home... to a relieved Anne.

16
HANGING IN

July 20

While waiting to explore this new possibility, I thought back to James Spring who was willing to be so generous in helping us, but was foiled by considerations of wisdom and prudence; and who a few days ago seemed to say he was withdrawing totally.

I thought it would be nice to comfort him with the thought that I had found another person who might help us instead. I told him the few details I knew about this Mike Hills.

But James again can't shirk off his involvement.
He reacted immediately and emailed: "The constant here, obviously, is that somebody needs to go in.

In an e-mail to a friend earlier this morning, I stupidly mentioned your positive e-mail, alluding to the 95% chance that my services would not be required. She was sage in her response, however. She said that you must care about me immensely to be trying to exhaust so many possibilities rather than still call on me.

She did not feel relieved; rather, she felt that it was only delaying the inevitable, and that one day soon, after you have tired of being jerked around by others, you will still ask me to go in.

I'm the man for the job. I hate it, too. But I'll tell you this: If I go into that jungle, I'm coming out. Just like I did last time, with great respect, humility, strength, speed, and awareness. I would be fully prepared to do limited checking in the fringe villages. Maybe we could find out many answers (names of guides, the last village entered, etc.). We might not, however, find out where the trail ends, and the details to be painted by the scene I envision.

And for reasons that even I don't fully understand, I believe the trail ends in the abandoned village of Payita, one day's hike from Arquia (one-and-a-half days from Paya). I feel that I must at least be prepared to go that far, whether or not we find it necessary for me to actually make the trek. This time, with the sat-phone and constant coordination of my position, also, with my registry with the US State Department I feel better backed than any expedition to enter previously.

I talked to my travel companion from the last trek. Regardless, he, too, lived through the Darien. Two days ago, he said to me, "There's a 97% chance you're going to be fine, but things happen. Planes crash. Trees fall." I agree with his assessment. I, more than anyone else, including the security company in Bogota, have the best chance of repeating my own success five months later.

If anything that I write here resonates with you, please weight up whether it is worth your while to embark on this obscure and time-consuming possibility. I am not going into the jungle to die. I am going so that I can live."

He also warned of the reliability of many people and their "economy with the truth". And he gave as an example that his brother told him about a man who had said that he had lived in the Darien for 25 years among the Indians. He had gone on more than 100 search and rescue missions. But when queried in detail about it, the guy changed his tune and said that he thinks he went once there for a holiday. All the rest was hallucination.

In other words: be wary, and don't believe anything you hear unless you have proof.

I take the admonition, but it is so frustrating dealing at third hand.

We passed on some of our correspondence with James Spring to the Hart Dykes, but their comment was, "Don't trust him. He is too good to be true."

17
SEARCHING FROM THE COLOMBIAN SIDE

July 19

A little backtrack about another search path – the detective agency in Bogota.

The Hart Dykes felt that if our side had flown out to Panama, then they should do something, so Sarah flew out to the Colombian capital, Bogota, just after the article in the *Times* was published.

But before flying she had managed to get the name of a detective or search agency in Bogota. It called itself "The total security company", and was said to have been operating for about 10 years. The company worldwide was said to employ 13,000 security professionals.

It proposed this schedule.

1)Gather information from Government entities and Agencies in Bogota.
2)Check with government agencies and hotels (!) in the area of disappearance.
3)Check with agents which have contacts with subversive groups.
4)Check with Pais Libre (paramilitaries), Colombian military, Red Cross, church missionary groups, British embassy, US Embassy, Colombia Police.
5)Check with hospitals. DAS, military bases, police sta-

tions, NGOs, restaurants etc. in the provinces of Choco and Antioquia.

The cost was calculated as 18 days at $500 per day.

We thought all of this was too vague, too like previous advisors in Bogota, who hadn't a clue what was happening in the Darien far away, and who had no contacts there. The Darien was about a 1/12th part of the provinces of Choco and Antioquia – so they would be looking for a needle in a haystack. And we did not like their involving the Colombian army or, worse, the dangerous paramilitaries who had murdered Indians and nuns at whim just recently. We asked the Hart Dykes not to give any of the names we had given them (e.g. the guides) to the paramilitaries, lest they moved in on one of their killing sprees.

And there was no evidence of them having contacts with subversive groups on the other side of the divide, i.e. FARC.

The Agency managed to get a hold of James Spring's contact details, and they tried to get him to do the detective work for them. But James Spring was hors de combat by this stage. They also said to James Spring that they did not intend to visit Arquia, the one place where they might find an answer.

Then they asked him for advice, and when James Spring mentioned Unguia, the agency had never heard of it. So even if James Spring had still been active, he would not have wanted to work with such amateurism.

18
THREE MONTHS OF CONFUSION

July 23

We now entered a few months of great confusion.

I was prevented from going to a place where I might find out the truth at limited risk – the village of Archya in the Columbian lowlands, where the probable guides might have ended up.

I was prevented partly by my knowing that a white man with minimal Spanish would not be likely to succeed, and partly by Anne, who worried about the danger.

James Spring was prevented by the worries of his wider family.

That inability to act made both me and my wife even more frustrated.

But we both had to admit that finding out what had happened was only a first step. The main problem was getting Paul and Tom out of the jungle alive, if they were there.

A reader will be able to follow the next 3 months more easily if I divide the narrative between three elements separately – my correspondence with the con-man, Mike Hills, and that with James Spring, our voluntary advisor, and that with the detective agency, which seemed at times as untrustworthy as the con-man.

The dates may flip back and forward in the triple narrative, and that may confuse the reader.

But I can guarantee that the reader will not be more confused than we were, with happenings in different spheres all
occurring at the same time.

19
GARBLED INFORMATION

July 22

I faxed Mike Hills the basic things that his man Pedro should concentrate on, which were the following.

The crooked policeman's information.

The names in the Panamian Police books on the River Tuira at a number of points, not only searching for the lads' names, but seeing who passed through at the same time, in order to identify the guides.

The storekeeper in Boca de Cupe, who knows everything that happens in the village and is likely to know the names of the guides and the boatman.

The gossip in Pucuro, who is again likely to know everything that happens there, and would know about the lads passing through, and who they were with.

The names of the two guides who lead the Americans through in January: it is likely that they will have heard of anything that happened between Paya and Unguia.

The likelihood of Payita being the incident place: i.e. the place where the lads were either captured or murdered.

Most of these facts were provided by James Spring; he is very useful.

And the insistence that he must use these gun-runner contacts of his, instead of a European coming in from outside, since mouths will close with a European.

Since he asked for a map, I also e-mailed him a map of the Darien area.

July 29

A week passed and there was no news from Mike Hills.

I phoned him, and he said that his man Pedro was occupied with the gun-running down in Puerto Obaldia in the last week, and that he had not yet moved on to the Darien Gap area.

However, there is nothing I can do.

I asked Mike Hills if he had got any further with the Traveller's Chequesenquiries with the American Express Office in England. He said he had no reply.

Mike Hills said, "Pedro is going to go to Payita with four people from the USA who know the area very well and have done this before. We have used them in the past. They are going to have a good look around.

Pedro is not getting much help, and it seems that the doors that he taps on stay closed, and that it is as if people had something to hide. He wants names of people who could help."

I e-mailed again and asked what Pedro had found out from the contacts I had given him, and complained about the vagueness of the information. It all sounded dodgy, but there might be an element of truth in it.

He replied: "As I told you Pedro is doing his very best and I've told him in one week I want him to go back and start from where we first planned to start, pay the money and get some results, but I also want a full report on what he has done with the names."

He obviously gets the message that I am getting impatient at the lack of results, and I asked what had happened to the Panamanian policeman and all that.

A week later he admitted that he was as much in the dark as to what exactly Pedro was doing as we were, and he said, "We'll give him one week more, and then we will ask him to go back to what I asked him to do in the first place, use bribes."

He is willing to meet me on English soil where I could easily set a police trap for him.

July 30

I reply to Mike Hills: "Your message is very obscure.

I am not sure that I understand who the 'he' & 'him' is in your fax.

If it is Pedro, then I can imagine mouths closing since he is a European.

I thought that the person doing the investigation was not going to be Pedro but this Panamanian policeman with his 'sidelines'.

I'm sure that if the boatman was approached by an insider he would know the names of the guides – but not if approached by an outsider.

On the general situation:

1) We started off this operation with the hints that this policeman had some knowledge of the case. Now there's less mention of him. Why?

2) I seem to be supplying the information. I had expected he would be.

3) At the beginning there was the mention of the Travellers' Cheques. Now all is silent about Travellers' Cheques.

4) I thought at first he was said to be a policeman located around Paya. Now the investigator hasn't been to Paya yet.

So I do not understand what has been happening. Are we going in the right direction? Pedro may be OK for a Payita visit, but not for confidential questioning."

It is funny that Mike Hills asks for clues – that I have to give him information, rather than he gives it to me. I repeat the information about the Police books on the river and the names of the village gossips.

20

STILL IN CONTACT

July 22

When I came back from Ostend, I had an email from James Spring waiting for me. He is fascinated still, but I am worried to involve him if his family is against it.

He said: "Avoiding emailing is good. We can do more of our normal jobs we are paid for..." But then: "Thanks for the offer of paying for flights, but I've essentially delegated involvement for a little time."

But I couldn't resist telling him the result of my visit to Ostend.

"I met the gun agent in Belgium near the Holland border, and though I could pick a few holes in him, I think that there is a reasonable chance that he is on to a genuine contact – a crooked Panamanian policeman – probably one of those who hadn't been answering the British Embassy because he was waiting for this opportunity. I think that this underworld will be far more likely to find out the truth than frontal probing from a white man.

And I will just add a bit to our philosophical discussion of about a week ago – about deliberately courting danger as an ego-boost and a bit of excitement. Of course it's true. You saw I put it more gently in the *Times* (those bits were written 6 weeks ago), 'Paul was shy at school, and perhaps his adventures were a part of his coming out of himself', or the pseudo-quotation 'I did it because I thought it would be a good story when I got home, and an achievement'... saying the same thing more gently...)

But it doesn't just apply to you or him; it applies to every growing person (and, less urgently, grown person). You were judging yourself too harshly.

Let's illustrate it in a different sphere.

One of my elder brothers was not academic, and my mother (who had little education and was therefore very keen on education) moved him from school to school – often at 6-monthly intervals – until he eventually left school and started off as a shop assistant. He was a contrast to the other 3 of us who were academic. Well, I believe that he spent his whole life proving to himself that she was wrong about his worth. In middle life he became the manager of a chain of mini-markets, and expanded it and made a great success of it. But even on a Sunday when we were there he'd be slipping off for part of the time to his job-cum-hobby, which was also his life. He rarely took his wife for holidays abroad. And he smoked and drank whiskey as a solution to the stress his overwork caused him (though I never saw him drunk). Anyway this weakened his heart and with some complications he died some years ago. But I'm convinced that his whole life's aim was to prove our mother wrong in her judgement about his ability – even long after she was dead.

But in case you think I am trying to prove myself 'wiser-than-thou' – God forbid, I believe that age makes no difference."

21

CONTRADICTORY STORIES

August 10

A week passed and Mike Hills came back with a garbled reply: "They are on the way back and are going to start with what I told them to do, also they have photos for me as soon as I have them you will have them the have found something but it is not for you but they say that something happened there not so long ago anyway they are as I say going back to square one so now as I wanted pay and lets get some results."

It seemed that he could spell and punctuate reasonably when he wanted to, but whenever he wanted to be obscure he went for bad spelling and punctuation.

And he said that the Panamanian policeman proved more crooked than he expected, and now didn't want to tell us anything.

All, of course, sounding very fishy, but I hung on in case there might be some element of truth in it – and there was no alternative source of knowledge at the time.

A week later I enquired again, and his reply was as obscure again: "My people are back and have been joined by three American missionaries that I contacted that make the same trip quite often and know of your lads and also are trusted by the locals they are starting out Friday of this week and will make contact with me through one of the churches in the USA on a weekly time or before if needed so now the group are 6 persons now so we should get some results the are going to see the people that you gave to me and also others that they know,"

I immediately e-mailed him back asking what church and what order the missionaries belonged to, and why he was again using whites who could find out nothing in that area, since we had agreed that only Indian contacts could obtain any real information, and why there is no information from the police books on the river... and again I ask for the Traveller's Cheques numbers.

He replied: "As I said they have gone back to the start and that the people they are now working with are 1 the policeman 2 the missionaries who have been working the area since 1991 the other persons are for protection only will send you more details when I am home the middle of next week . So the three missionaries have turned into the policeman (resurrected suddenly) and two missionaries, and he didn't answer what church they belong to or give their names. And there were these 3 other mysterious Americans there "for protection".

And was he selling guns or buying guns in Japan?
And on the number of the Traveller's Cheques, no word.

But strange to say he claimed he hasn't passed over any money yet. He could easily have spun a yarn saying that he had passed over money, and I would not be any the wiser. But perhaps he did not dare say it, since he had found out no information.

August 13

Still no word came back from Mike Hills about that "person in Pucuro who would have something for him last Monday or Tuesday" or "the name of the boatman that the local shopkeeper was going to give to him" or the photos of Payita. On the last we wanted especially to see the photographs to let James Spring recognise whether it was genuinely Payita or not.   ·

I complained to Mike Hills about the lack of information, and at the Panamian policeman suddenly disappearing off the scene.

It will be obvious to the reader that I only continued on in a desperate desire for certainty, when there was no other source of viable information. My wife, Anne, asked me to stop phoning Mike Hills since there was no rhyme or reason in most of his statements.

It was also becoming obvious that with the advent of internet, fake news was very

easy to invent. Every American in 2016 knows that well.

22
CLOSER TO THE CONMAN VERDICT

August

Back-tracking on James Spring: a dog worrying a bone.

I have said that the months of July and August moving into September was a period of great confusion.

All sources of investigation had dried up except Mike Hills, so, to keep hope alive, we "had to" at least partly believe him. But much of what he said was contradictory or inconsistent.

Of course, in hindsight, I should have added two and two together and realised the deceit earlier.

James Spring, even though he was prevented from participating in the search itself, tried to help me by checking on the veracity of what Mike Hills was saying.

James said: "Get him to take some photos of Payita.

Payita has some clearly recognizable features. I would like to hear or see what they saw so that I might be able to confirm whether or not they went. It's a lonely, deadly, and arduous trek. Payita is a half-day from the Colombian border at the top of Cerro Tugun.

Coincidentally, why did Mike want to help? Is he a father, too? I have to believe that he has good intentions. From what do they arise?"

I replied: "We'll try this chap for a while yet. The problem is that Mike says that Pedro is "his man", but how much "his man" I don't know.

You asked as to why I trust Mike: Well, I don't fully, but he's a reasonable chance – or seemed so at first.

Some reasons:

1) He has a selfish motive: people out there need money to buy his guns: if a fellow out there can earn money from me for information, then he will have money to buy a few of Mike's guns.

2) The father motive: he did say that he had a daughter missing out East a few years ago.

3) He gave me good proof of his address in Holland, which I could use against him.

4) When he (or rather Pedro) seemed to be getting nowhere a few days ago, he simply offered me my money back."

A week later, James comes back again: "Don't give up on Paul yet. It's like a poker game. Enough is invested in the pot. It's worth seeing the final card."

And the week later: "Just a quick note to touch bases and let you know that your family remains in the forefront of my thoughts and hopes".

23

MORE FAR-FETCHED CLAIMS

Again, dear reader, if you want to skip this chapter, then do so.

For us to listen to these far-fetched narrations was painful and this book is not designed to cause the same pain for you.

September 4

I have contacted Mike Hills again, and he replies very briefly: "THE ONLY NEWS I HAVE FOR YOU AT THIS MOMENT IS THAT THE PEOPLE SAY THEY ARE STILL WORKING AND THAT THEY HAVE NOT MADE A GREAT DEAL OF PROGRESS AND THAT THING TAKE TIME TO GET GOOD RESULTS AND THAT THE LOCAL PEOPLE WONT BE RUSHED BUT THINGS ARE MOVING EVEN THOUGH IT IS NOT FAST AS WE WANT IT TOO. I WILL KEEP YOU UP WITH THE LATEST AS I GET THINGS TO ME SPEAK TO YOU SOON."

September 8

I have pressed Mike Hills again for news, and said more directly in an e-mail: "When you first approached me you indicated that your contacts had information available, and even if it was not there for the asking, it was 'there for the paying of a bribe'. You are now basically admitting that you are not in contact with anyone who has any information at all".

This provoked a reply from Mike, the same day.

"BRIAN,
MAY BE GOOD OR NOT I HAVE SO FAR PAID
175000$ AND LIKE YOU GOT NOTHING APART FROM
ONE PERSON DEAD WHO WAS ASKING QUES-
TIONS IN THE WRONG PLACE AT THE WRONG TIME
ABOUT THE GUIDES SO ARE THEY PART OF A GANG
OR WHAT
YOU TELL ME, ALL I CAN DO AT THE MOMENT IS
WAIT TO SEE WHAT IS GOING ON
I DO KNOW THAT THE FRIEND OF YOUR SON WAS
NOT DOING THE RIGHT THING HE WAS TRANS-
PORTING SOMETHING THAT YOUR SON DID NOT
KNOW ABOUT AND FOR THAT HE PAID THE PRICE
WHAT PRICE WE DON'T KNOW. YOU SEE BRIAN
I AM TRYING BREAK A DRUG RING THAT YOUR
BOYS AS I THOUGHT WOULD BE WORKING WITH
BUT IT SEEMS THAT YOUR BOY NEW NOTHING
ABOUT IT.I WOULD BE BETTER TO SPEAK ON THE
PHONE THAN LIKE THIS. PHONE ME AT HOME
WHEN YOU RECEIVE THIS EMAIL
MIKE."

These enigmatic messages were turned into plain English
on Mike's mobile phone conversation (which my wife Anne
also listened to as follows): "One of the lads was carrying
$475,000 as a drugs settlement. The guides were part of a
gang involved in this business. They brought the lads to
Payita where one of them handed over the cash. The other
started asking questions because he hadn't known about this
up to that point, and the gang killed him, and whisked the
other away to a hideout, where he still is.

Pedro was given a tip in Paya to go to Pucuro where a

contact would tell the names of the guides for a sum of money. Pedro was warned not to go alone, but he went and was killed there."

So, suddenly, two reported deaths. Fishy.

Mike said he tried to phone the police in Panama City about the murder of Pedro, but they put the phone down. He also told us about the involvement of his sister with this same drug gang.

The Drugs Enforcement Agency had been trailing one of the lads for a long time, and had other instances against him. A missionary named Tim Wyma was one of Mike's informants. Mike was on the payroll of the Drugs Enforcement Agency, and he was meeting two members of the DEA in Dover on Monday 11th September.

September 10

I had asked to attend this meeting of Mike Hills and the DEA in Dover to try to get an answer to some of my questions, but Mike says that his DEA contact Martin does not want me present. He is willing to meet me after the meeting, however, about 3 pm. I suggest that we meet in a police station, but he says that the DEA would not like that, and he suggests that we meet in a café.

He suggested he will come over next weekend if that does not leave enough time.

Strange, the story is so full of holes and contradictions, but he is willing to meet me on English soil.

I agreed to meet him.

We asked many questions: how did Mike speak to the police in Panama City if he didn't speak Spanish? Etc.

I was suspicious of the story and I started asking questions of the British Embassy in Panama to try to confirm at least about Tim Wymer.

I typed the questions out and headed the piece "Mike's Story" with a great deal of scepticism. I was content that, if these questions could be satisfactorily answered, then I would believe the story. Otherwise, I would not.

Anne took a different attitude, and simply wrote out reasons why the story could not be true, and she listed the following.

Tom was expansive and open in his cards home. He was not the kind of shifty character who would be involved in drugs or money laundering.

Tom had no need of money. He had an inheritance to go back to.

Tom's passion was for trees and orchids. That kind of person would not be involved in drugs.

He did not instigate the trip down the Darien Gap. If he had an assignment, then he would have been fixed on it, and probably would not have wanted a companion to spy on him.

Paul also had shown complete openness about accepting anyone to go with him, and he e-mailed to many people seeking a companion. A person with an assignment would not do that.

They both said that they were prepared to change routes if it looked too dangerous. How could they meet their contacts with that flexible attitude?

If Mike has been trailing this gang which was responsible for his daughter's or sisters death, and if that death occurred in the East, why had it taken 10 years to track this gang down – and find it in the West?

If he was really searching for those who killed his sister or his daughter, why had he asked us for $7,500 to finance that search?

Why use white Europeans in an area where they are so conspicuous? Wouldn't the gang be far more likely to use a Spanish-American or an Indian?

Somehow or other, although Mike didn't convince us of his stories, he did for a short while convince us that the DEA could be involved.

And, of course, if the DEA was involved, then it could be operating secretly.

For one one two days I got the obsession that our phone might be tapped and I told our friend, Jenny Gillam, and the detective agency in Colombia about it.

24
A MEETING IN DOVER

September 11

As agreed a few days before, I met Mike Hills in Dover today. He confirmed and expanded on his story, and parried my questions very convincingly, but to many of them he said, "You will have to ask the DEA people that." In general, he was so convincing that I believed his story could possibly be true.

He promised to arrange a meeting in the immediate future.

To some of the other questions, he gave a plausible answer. And, of course, there was the excuse, "Pedro knew that one, but he is dead now."

He also said that this drug gang that was involved with the lads was the one that killed his daughter and kidnapped his sister (note that the story is expanding: at the first meeting his daughter had just gone missing out East. Now the story was that his sister had disappeared because of a drug gang, and his daughter had been killed in London by the same gang, not out East) and that he had spent $175,000 trailing this drug gang over the years.

He said he knew the name of the head of the gang, but there was no use pursuing that man because he was too powerful.

He also said that he always carried a gun with him.

He also changed his story about the money. Up to this meeting he said that he was still holding the money I gave him, and that none of it had been handed over for information. Now he said that he had handed over the $7,500 to the DEA, and they were holding it.

He also talked about his being hard up for money, and thought he might approach a newspaper to earn a bit with an article. I didn't suspect blackmail and I took it on its face value, and I said it would be no harm for him to try.

He suggested another meeting with the DEA people to include me – to be held in the UK probably on Friday 15th September.

25

UK POLICE & MIKE HILLS

We began to review all that had gone on previously and started to realise it was almost certainly lies from the beginning.

We made a list of the 18 reasons for this judgement, but in brief they amounted to: his so-called gun-running which he later denied, his many claims of getting information in Pucuro (which fizzled out), the photos of Payita (which never matured), the three American missionaries who, when challenged, turn into two missionaries (one, a very old man living near Panama City, who couldn't possibly travel through the Darien), the "rehabilitated" crooked policeman, his stories about drug-running through the gap (which US Intelligence sources said never happened because too arduous and difficult), the tall stories about $475,000 and the DEA, the murder of Pedro and one of the lads – his stories getting more and more unlikely as time went by.

Mike often reported on Pedro going to do something "over the next few days" but when I chased him on it a week later, Mike had forgotten what he had said the week before.

What kept me deceived for so long was his giving me his address, phone number and passport photocopies, electricity bills, etc., at the very beginning.

However, we had had enough and we went to the Chelmsford police, and reported the whole story.

We planned with the police to try to persuade Mike Hills to come over to England, so that they could arrest him.

Mike Hills was still talking about introducing me to the Drugs Enforcement Agency people and I suggested we meet at the Miami Hotel in Chelmsford.

We discussed with the police the possibility of them arresting him there if he appeared, but they were rather worried by the fact that Mike Hills had said that he always carried a gun on him. Would they surround the hotel with armed police?

But they need not have worried. Mike Hills made excuses for not coming.

Finally, the police got us to make a full statement about Mike Hills' fraud, which they could keep as evidence for their prosecuting him if he should ever come to England and they could arrest him.

26 How to Challenge Statutory Incompetence

We have not said much to the Hart Dykes about Mike Hills, because from the beginning we did not really trust him.

We just followed every report he came up with and tried to see if there could be some element of truth in it. We are constantly puzzled as to why he has been so open about his personal details and so prompt of response both over the phone and email – not the normal con-man who grabs the money and runs.

But now that we are slowly coming to the conclusion that everything he has said is lies, we have communicated this to James Spring. He does not just reply, but puts a whole new plan of action into place.

September 18

"I was ecstatic to receive your e-mail and would like to give it a better response than what I am currently capable of.

Needless to say, we are ecstatic that your eyes are enjoying a broader perspective. Whatever the truths end up being, you can only benefit by the questions you will now be asking.

We are relieved beyond words. I would have hated making my return trip to Europe a vengeful one in search of a potentially dangerous Dutchman with an unusually common name. I'm glad knowing I can sleep and that you are well in control of protecting yourself.
I'll write more in the am
James"

My reaction to that is: how generous of James Spring. He should have called me a bloody fool.

September 19

On the next day James wrote: "Why can't the following be done?
Meet with a London Interpol representative. Let them know that you are holding their feet to the fire – no excuses.

Monitor progress between Interpol London and Interpol Panama. Check daily to see what has been done. One objective should be to find the location of the PNP books. If they are still in the jungle, we need a document giving us permission to visit the PNP garrisons along the Tuira, and check the registries. The concept seems so ludicrous in the first world that we inhabit, but this type of thing happens often in Central America. I would travel to Boca de Cupe (or Pucuro). This way I avoid the dangers of Colombia. Nobody is safer in a Kuna village than I am.

If I am not allowed to go solo, a PNP agent from Panama City should be assigned to us. Send me with the agent. We could fly to El Real and do all of the stops in one day. I could talk to Tocallo in Boca de Cupe. Then I could continue on to Pucuro alone or with the PNP officer. (It might be safer alone, though.) I could ask the questions to the people I already know in Pucuro (and meet nobody new).

In the absence of Interpol's intervention, schedule a meeting with the Panamanian consulate. (Do I need to be there? Or could/should I attend by telephone on a speaker phone so that I can explain the geography in the greatest detail?) Secure info about location of PNP books from the 4 cuarteles along the Tuira. If the books are in the jungle, our objective is to get a typed and sealed document that could be presented to the sergeant in each garrison along the way.

This sounds even more ludicrous than the scenario presented above, but this is the way I have travelled through much of Latin America. Once I went to the Costa Rican Consulate in Los Angeles and pulled a similar stunt. I needed to bring a car into Costa Rica. I saw that the sign on the wall said that the Consulate offered documents bearing the official seal for $15 US. I wrote down exactly what I needed the document to say. They typed it up, sealed it and took my $15.

When I arrived in Costa Rica the immigration and customs officials looked at the paper, never having seen anything like it, and waved me immediately through as a dignitary.

This could play even easier in the remote jungles of Panama. The protocol intended by Panama City's PNP headquarters is subject to interpretation by the outposts. I feel that I could (and have had to in the past) create my own document to allow me access to the books. But we need to find out where they are first.

I wish that this challenge was all based in the US rather than in England.

I know how to play our game. I don't know how well it translates in the UK.

I'll make some calls to the Panamanian Consulate here just in case.

Are you up for any of this?
Do you want me to back off?
What do you want?

So you now have the option: fight or flight.

If I know you at all, you're not about to fly. Let's get in and resolve this. I'm on your team. Be the captain; I'm happy to follow.

Doubt your emotions, trust your intellect. We can make room for emotions later.

Contrary to what would appear obvious, your open admission and genuine apology (which I know that you want to extend)to the Hart Dykes will give you greater power and bring you closer to working with them.

What can The American do for us? And why hasn't he called me yet?

Let's stop wasting time on past mistakes. I am still proud to have you lead the charge.

Ready. Able. Willing. James"

September 27

James Spring went to the Panamanian Consulate in Anaheim and told the consul the whole story, and asked him to find out why no information was coming from the Panama police. It seems that the consul was very considerate and welcoming.

It transpires that the Panamanian police did open a file on the incident, but that it came to a standstill because they did not have the passport numbers or the location where the lads entered Panama originally.

But I gave these facts to the British embassy months ago to be given to the Panama police. I can't be bothered finding the details again among my e-mails. Nothing will come of it anyway, since the Panamanian police are only interested in how the lads entered the country, not how they left it.

James was thinking of putting a request through the American Embassy, even though that institution does not normally get involved with people who are not US citizens.

James is proposing to invent the passport numbers and the points of entry as a means of getting the police moving. He is also e-mailing the Minister of Justice, the President and a journalist with La Prensa in Panama, called Herasto Reyes. It seems that he is a poet and a good writer with true compassion. I will let him do that to see if anything can come of it.

He also says that by reading the Panamian press he has learned that the situation has been growing worse: "Armed Colombian rebels swooped down from the jungle in mid-February and opened fire on the PNP outpost in Union Choco. More Panamanians have disappeared. Colombian rebels have become brazen, attending dances in the indigenous communities, drinking booze in the humble eateries of Boca de Cupe. They have no fear of the PNP.

Residents and merchants were quoted about the satisfaction they have experienced in their business dealings with the rebels."

27
THE JAPAN DECEIT

September

Our friend, Jenny Gillam (see June 3rd) noticed some time ago that Mike Hills had mentioned in one of his memos that he was in Japan, and she reminded me of the fact that the article about Lucie Blackman the 21-year-old missing in Japan had appeared on the same page in the *Times* as my article about Paul & Tom on July 19th.

It seemed a possibility, so I used 192.com to find Lucie's address in Sevenoaks. There were two other people at the same address, Jane and Sophie, Lucie's mother and sister. I couldn't find a phone number for the same address, so after work I decided to drive down without warning. I was asked in by Jane. I simply asked, "Did you have a person from Holland offering to help you in the search for Lucie?"
Jane said, "Yes, a Mike Hills. Most of us think he's a con-man."
Yippee. I've at least done one thing right recently.

They told me that Lucie's father had gone along with Mike Hill's stories in the hope that there might be some truth in them – like myself – but Jane did not believe him from the first. But like us, there was the pain of not knowing. I sympathised with them. I could do no more.

The Blackman's were reported as having handed over more money than we did to Mike Hills. And it was reported that Mike Hills was more cruel to them also, persuading the father to come out to meet him in Hong Kong to pick up information about Lucie. But I never found out if that was true or not.

It was obvious that that article in the *Times* in July was the source of Mike Hills contacting both of us.

28
MIKE HILLS: SURREAL FANTASY

September 20

We've had another interview with the police, this time with the Fraud Squad. We've given them a statement with all the facts and background of Mike Hills.

We asked for a recording device to be fitted to our phone, but it seems that it is quite difficult to arrange. They have to get the permission of the Head of Police in Essex, and fill in all kinds of paperwork before that can happen – all because of this obsession with privacy – even though we, the house-holders, had actually requested it, and the correspondent was outside the UK!

After 2 weeks of delay, eventually a basic tape-recorder was fixed to our phone. We had naively thought that phone calls could be intercepted at the central exchanges and re-corded, but seemingly Essex Police were unaware of any such sophisticated method. Anyway, after that recorder was installed, we recorded many conversations with Mike Hills as he invented more stories and wriggled to get out of an-swering any questions.

The purpose of continuing emails and phone calls with Mike Hills was to gather evidence for a criminal trial and to try to persuade him to come to England so that the police could arrest him.

All kinds of conversations with Mike Hills continued, and I will mention a few to indicate the kind of pressure that this kept us under with no prospect of contributing to a solution in finding Paul:

I noticed in the papers today (September 20th) that a Luke Dance had disappeared in the Yonga region of Bolivia. It gave the name of the police officer who is dealing with the case in Crawley. Mike Hills phoned me about it off his own bat, and it was obvious that he was thinking of getting money out of this family also on pretence of searching for their son. I phoned the police officer in Crawley to warn him of the possibility.

I queried with Mike Hills about these DEA (Drug Enforcement Agency) officers he promised to introduce me to and he would come over to Dover on 21st to introduce me to them. Early in the morning he phoned to say that he could not make it because he said that he was blocked on the motorway in Holland by a blockage of diesal-price protesters and could not make it.

He asked for a suggestion from me as to where we could meet on the next day to introduce the DEA officers and I suggested at the Miami hotel in Chelmsford. He agreed and he even suggested that he could bring the $7500 to refund to me. I mentioned this to the police and asked if they were willing to attend, but when they heard that he had said that he always carried a gun with him they were hesitant because of all the bureaucracy there would be for an armed officer to be there. They need not have worried. He made up another excuse for not coming.

When I queried Mike Hills about the DEA people again, he replied. This is the reply and it is fairly typical: "BRIAN,

THE REASON FOR THE MEETING IS TO GIVE YOU THE MONEY BACK AND TO SAY THAT THE DEA WILL NOT WORK WITH YOU UNDER YOUR TERMS AND THAT YOU MUST UNDERSTAND THAT THE DEA IS NOT A PRIVATE COMPANY. IF YOU WANT TO CONTINUE THEN YOU MUST WAIT FOR THE RESULTS THAT WILL COME IN CONCERNING YOUR SON AND UNDERSTAND THAT MANY THINGS CANNOT BE TOLD TO YOU BECAUSE IT COULD MAKE THE JOB HARDER. I WILL BE ABLE TO GIVE YOU REPORTS FROM THEM WHEN I GET THEM AND NOT BEFORE, I HAVE SENT YOUR E,MAILS TO THEM AS I HAVE RECIVED THEM AND THEY THINK THAT YOU HAVE CHANGED AND HAVE BECOME VERY DEMANDING."

I replied that I was not demanding anything I did not ask for from the beginning: this information from the DEA of the lads handling drugs and drug money was a very serious accusation, and the claim that one of them had been killed was as serious, and he had to justify them.

We arranged another meeting in Dover for 28th, but again he did not turn up. He sent this message: "BRIAN. AFTER SITTING UP MOST OF THE NIGHT WAITING FOR A CALL I STILL DONT KNOW WHAT IS GOING ON SO PLEASE DONT EVEN ASK. I HAVE NOT HAD ANY PHONE CALLS OR ANY OTHER KIND OF MESAGE. I AM GOING TO TRY SOMTHING ON MY OWN BACK AND TRY TO GET IN TOUCH WITH A DEA OFFICE IN THE U.S.TO SEE IF THEY CAN HELP US I SHALL ALSO ASK FOR YOU TO BE EMAILED ALONG WITH MYSELF WITH ANY RESULT. SO AGAIN IT LOOKS VERY BAD ON ME FOR MAKING THE MEETING BUT

ITS NOT MY FAULT.I DO KNOW THAT ONE OF THEM WENT TO PANAMA I ALSO KNOW THAT THEY GOT SOMTHING BUT I DONT KNOW WHAT,IT IS LIKE THEY ARE NOW KEEPING ME IN THE DARK.AGAIN BRIAN I,M SORRYFOR THE MESS.I WILL SPEAK TO YOU WHEN I RECIVE NEWS FROM MY E,MAIL TO THEM. MIKE. P/S I HAVE JUST HEARD THE WEATHER NEWS IT LOOKS AS THOUGH I WOULD NOT HAVE MADE IT TODAY MANY FERRY BOATS CANCELED." Of course, they were not cancelled...

October 2

Mike's next trick was to email me to say that a DEA contact in Panama called Philipe would phone me. He added: "This Philipe is foreign. I think he's from Panama. I'm not sure. He said he'd phone Brian tomorrow night. I didn't know what for and I asked, 'What do you want to speak to Brian for?' He wouldn't tell me: 'No, I want to speak to Mr Winder.' Oh, well, he told me his name was Philip because I'd find out what he wanted. Well, he's in Panama, I think: that's the guy who went to Panama. Apparently, he's one of the gang who's supposed to come to a meeting with Brian. He wants to speak to Brian. He wouldn't speak to me. He wouldn't tell me anything. I haven't got a clue what he wants to talk about. I know who Philip is. I've met him once. But, eh, as I say, I don't know what he want to speak to Brian about. He won't speak to me."

I then got a phone-call from this so-called Philipe who claimed to be phoning from Panama and who offered to meet me outside the American Embassy in Canada in a few days' time. Of course, I did not go.

October 9

I got this message from this so-called Philipe: "MR WINDER I SHALL BE SENDING YOU SOME PHOTO-GRAPHS OF SOME THINGS WE HAVE FOUND ALONG WITH SOME OTHER DETAILS WE WOULD LIKE TO YOU TO STUDY WHAT WE SEND YOU TO SEE IF YOU CAN IDENTIFY ALL OR SOME OF THE THINGS. AT A LATER DATE YOU MAY HAVE TO COME TO PANA-MA TO LOOK AT WHAT WE HAVE FOUND. I SHALL TELEPHONE YOU IN THE NEXT WEEK. PHILIPE."

I could continue the narrative of these communications for another 5 or 6 pages.

The reader may wonder why I still corresponded with Mike Hills when we had decided that all he said was lies. It was obvious that this Philipe was just Mike Hills trying to put on the accent of a Spaniard speaking English badly, and his email address was just invented for the occasion.

The reason I continued was mainly to try to entice him to come over to the UK to be arrested, which was a valid reason.

But there were probably a few other subconscious moti-vations : (1) to get my own back on him by pestering him to invent tall stories (2) a fascination of the kind of paralysis that a small animal is said to suffer when a stoat is about to kill it and (3) because nothing valid was moving on any oth-er front in solving the problem of Paul going missing.

One of the convincing reasons was that Mike was obses-sively telling lies and had made up the existence of "Philipe" was that anyone who knows the Spanish-speaking world would know that the name would be spelt "Filipe". So Mike not only made up the name, but set up an email address for him using "Philipe".

Another interesting thing: We had discovered that Mike Hills did indeed meet someone on the 11th September in Dover, but that it was not the DEA, but probably the police, and that he was acting as an informer to them. You may be sure that the information he fed them was as false as that which he fed us.

October 17

I made a further statement to the police with the most recent evidence.

Anne became too distraught with these phone-calls and wanted an end to them. She could not bear the lies and deceit, and to be honest, we had gathered enough evidence against Mike Hills without this torture continuing. So I told Mike Hills what I thought of him in an e-mail – but only about his promising information and not giving it, not about his being an out-and-out con-man. Then there followed a resulting angry phone conversation, and that ended contact with Mike Hills. It was mid-October.

29
THE LADS ARE NO LONGER ALIVE

November

The Hart Dykes after their using the detective Agency in Bogota and returning home suggested that we might like to join them in using a connected detective agency in Panama – whose boss was an American who had good contacts with the Panama police. We will cause that person "The American".

Despite his being in this very privileged position, we will see that he was initially no better than the Bogota detective agency or indeed Mike Hills.

Early October.

The American's initial blurb sounded excellent.

He would: "1) Get the director of the National Police to let me get a look at the local record books in Puerto Obaldia, Boca de Cupe, Pucuro and Paya. These are the only places the lads would have been logged in that will provide a trail to follow. Books in these areas are haphazardly maintained, frequently 'corrected', reused, etc., but they may tell us as much by what they don't contain as by what they do.

2) Send one of my investigators to Puerto Obaldia to verify the sighting of two young white men, and find out when and how the lads left. This investigator would be an ex-military era officer who is now a public force officer and func-

tions as one of my intelligence specialists. He is experienced in field information collection and will be respected by the local police garrison.

3) Follow up and verify the information provided by the Kuna in June. I have a man who is from the area and is going on vacation this week. He is experienced, lives in the area, knows the local population and has a reason to be there. I want him to talk to the family that the lads stayed the night with in Boca de Cupe, track down the cayuco driver who took them up river, verify if there were guides or not and attempt to trace them as far as Paya."

And he added: "My lads are trained in information collection and are from that area of the Darien. They are also public force officers, which will give them the access with the police that others would not have. They have all of the names, photos and previous lead info to go on with. Hopefully we will learn something."

He also said that he himself was an expert at everything to do with the jungle. He had been a US Navy SEAL Commander, working in the jungles of South-East and Central America for many years and had lived in Panama since 1984. He also had a contact returning from Boca de Cupe on the day he initially contacted us.

We agreed with the Hart Dykes to share the cost of employing him.

All that sounded very encouraging – at first.
Many of the ideas, however, were copied from James Spring's suggestions to the Colombian detective agency.
James Spring offered to help in the exercise – at least to

the extent of briefing anyone who would work on the case.

The American, however, soon became very anti-James Spring, and I am sure it was because James Spring showed himself to be far more knowledgeable about the Darien than these so-called "professionals".

We will also see that in the end that the Agency failed to carry out most of the tasks promised.

In early October The American came up with this momentous information: "I received information from a contact that has been reliable in the past that indicates that the lads ARE NO LONGER ALIVE. So far, this is an unconfirmed report and we're working to resolve some inconsistencies but I give it some credibility for the following reasons.

On the Puerto Obaldia side: I have talked at length with an agent of the Colombian detective agency who went to Capurganá and Puerto Obaldia. He met with the hotel owner in Capurganá who identified the pictures of Tom and Paul, and took the same cayuco that took the lads to Puerto Obaldia.

According to the agent, both the hotel owner and boat operator were positive in their identification. The same with 6-8 people in Puerto Obaldia who were positive in their identification of the lads and their tent/gear.
After two to three days they just got up and disappeared."

The American the next day said: "Today, I debriefed our reliable contact, who works for us in the Darien, upon his return from several weeks in Boca de Cupe.

At my request, he sought out and talked to the family that

the lads stayed with and talked to the canoe operator that they hired. The woman 'Dori' remembered them, and her cousin was the canoe operator that the lads hired. He tells us that he warned them that it was very dangerous to go to Paya (South East) and took them to Yape (North) and that they did not have any guides with them."

This version totally contradicts the original story of the Indian I sent up the Gap, Margarito Rosales.

The American continued: "All of this information, if credible, bolsters the theory that the lads heeded the warnings and turned north. They probably took the old route north from Yape that goes up into the Panama Darien National Park. This park is pretty much abandoned and overgrown because of the guerrilla threat but here is where the orchids are, in the high cloud rain forest.

It is a rough trip, takes 10 days to 2 weeks and not for the faint of heart or lightly equipped. This would explain the lads' appearance in Capurganá.
Puerto Obaldia, 20 minutes by boat from Capurgana, is the closest point of access to transportation to Panama or Turbo.

Conclusions: I believe the lads were in Pto. Obaldia. They did not have enough money to fly back to Panama or get a boat to Turbo so they tried to walk back to Yaviza. They were either taken from the town or along the border.
I do not believe the police in Pto. Obaldia were directly involved but they probably have some knowledge of what happened to the boys. This will be very difficult to prove.

Panama will not admit the extent of the problem to its own citizens and publicly denies the presence of large guerrilla forces in Panama, even when provided precise locations and details."

So, The American's story was that the lads were dead and that somehow they did not go through the Centre of the Darien Gap.

The stories had very much the ring of a Mike Hills' story.

We shall see later that both of these pieces of "information" from The American were totally false.

Having been schooled by the Mike Hills affair, we were rather sceptical of The American's "facts".

Coached by James Spring, I replied to The American on the different points: "There are definite inconsistencies: Tom was a communicator and sent 3 cards from Yaviza, so he would have sent one from Puerto Obaldia before going back into the jungle which you suggested happened.

Also the 'no money' suggestion does not ring true: Paul took $300 out in Yaviza, and Sarah Hart Dyke said that Tom took out over $1,000, so how can $1,300 have got spent in a week in the jungle? Paul was very economic with money.

And I pestered him again: "Have you checked if their names appear in the police books anywhere?"

The American replied on that point: "The 'no money' angle didn't add up to me either."

I also copied the information to James Spring, and he came forward with more cogent arguments. Remember he had said he wanted to opt-out of the whole investigation a few days ago, but he can't resist an intellectual challenge. He replied with his usual concern.

"Firstly, I appreciate your concern about bothering me. However, I am so involved in the resolution of this sad affair, I regard it as no trouble.

The American's hypothesis would say that your original Indian guide Margarito was lying: i.e. that the lads never made it to Paya. Not even to Pucuro.

Secondly, in order to get from Boca de Cupe back to Yape, the lads would have had to have signed in twice in police book in Capeti, since Capeti is upriver of Yape and between Yape and Boca de Cupe. The Panamian Police books of Capeti would certainly show this. The Capeti garrison is on a bluff over the Tuira river. All piraguas must stop and register.

So this hypothesis must not be put forward without checking the police books at Capeti.

The high cloud forest in which orchids are found is not found only along the path as the letter from The American alludes. Panama and Colombia are separated by a mountain range that spans the entire isthmus, and the whole area would have a similar high cloud forest.

I don't know if both lads had what it took to get all the way through to Capurgana on foot. I can also promise you that had there been a hotel available in Pto Obaldia, the lads after spending the nightmarish time in the jungle would never have opted to camp another night in a field. This is not a pleasant walk by any standard. So The American's hypothesis falls down.

A Panamanian Police registry check is absolutely necessary. What do the books say? It is the only thing which might be relied upon.

You are paying The American. Tell him that you are not interested in recovering clues in Obaldia. Tell him the only thing that you are interested in is seeing what the Panamian Police books say. It is the easiest task of all. And the longer we take, the better chance that the books will be lost, and the soldiers who entered the info will be reassigned elsewhere".

After James' points I said rather more forcibly to The American: "Thanks for the communications.
The stay in Capurgana and Puerto Obaldia does not make sense.
They had plenty of hard cash (if they had been robbed earlier, they would have reported it to the police).

Airplane flights accept credit cards, and airplane flights are dirt cheap by European standards in Panama. Paul had at least $5,000 credit available on his card, as well as American Express Travellers' Cheques, which are almost cash.

The hotels also are dirt cheap, and after coming out of the hellish week or 10 days trek in the jungle, they would certainly not have camped on the football pitch.

They were both heading South; Paul hoped to be clear of Colombia in two weeks. Why would they choose to go back through the jungle?
Why do their names not appear in the police book in Puerto Obaldia?
You yourself do not fully trust Gomez since he told a lie about contacting Paya by phone.

If the lads were lounging around in Puerto Obaldia as described, Tom would certainly have sent a card.

So, it all doesn't make sense.

Now as to what must be the urgent points, the Panamanian Police books. First confirm that Paul & Tom's names appear in the books of Capeti twice: on the way to Boca de Cupe, and on the way downriver from Boca de Cupe (through Capeti) to Yape, possibly one on 11th March and on 12th March or after. This would confirm their journey downriver at least.

If there was a question of a return journey later over the same route (all the way from Puerto Obaldia?!), the same books would be useful."

The American is strangely silent about these Panamanian Police books. Obviously they are a state secret, or he has not sent anyone to check and he cannot get at them. And he depended too much on his agent.

The American then went on to assert: "There is no bank in Obaldia and no one will accept cheques there. It is cash only.

I don't mean to sound melodramatic but most of us in the civilised world think these kinds of places exist only in the movies."

Jams Spring countered this with: "Traveller's Cheques can be changed in the small villages in the jungle. Even in tiny Unguia there were merchants who offered the service of trading our cheques for Colombian pesos. Even our guides took Traveller's Cheques."

The American then rambled on about his trying to get inside the lads' minds – a task that he was particularly unsuited for, which fortunately he soon dropped.

So James Spring directly contradicts The American about many of the facts. I know which of the two, James or the American, I would trust as reliable. James Spring without question.

James went on: "We must search the Panamian Police books of Puerto Obaldia around that time – not for Paul and Tom's names – but for any other European-style names. If any other European names are there, we could probably trace them down, and establish the likelihood or not of a mistaken identity.
Also get at the Capeti police books as quickly as possible before they disappear."

The American then starts defending himself, and it seems he is aware of James Spring and his analyses being behind what I was saying.
"Unlike James Spring, I have spent more than 34 years in the jungles of South East Asia, Central/South America and West Africa. During that time I have been shot three times, cut once, bitten by everything that walks, crawls, or talks and lost my fascination for the majesty of the noble savage."

I was tempted to reply but stopped myself.

All of this was a sure sign that our detective was getting rattled by our finding holes in nearly all his arguments.
He was right to be rattled. We will see later that all his facts were false.
We were reminded of Mike Hills.

In late October, The American came out with the information that he had confirmed that the lads had gone to Yape – for what it was worth.

At this stage everything looked very bleak, early November is a traditional time to think of the dead. We discuss the possibility of having a commemorative Mass for Paul's life, but delayed it.

I think of all the soldiers who were reported "missing in action" in the awful battles of the First World War, and how their parents were never able to grieve with certainty for them.

There is a desperate desire to know what happened.

30
INFORMATION FROM A FARC CAPTIVE

November 10

More nagging from James Spring on the Panamanian police books on the river.
It all helps.

November 11

Anne keeps asking, "What are we paying The American for?"

He has obviously been going off on tangents. I think he is honest, but he is failing to find out anything, that is because he cannot get in contact with the right sources.

I am content to wait.

I write an e-mail to the Hart Dykes to sound out their opinion on The American, but mainly to please Anne.

November 15

By mid-November The American's privileged position of contact with the Police started to pay dividends.

He reported: "Last week in Panama two Indians were picked up who are members of the FARC guerrillas. They were brought to Panama City a few days ago and have been co-operating with the authorities. They were asked if they had any knowledge of the two British lads lost last March... they said that two white people of that description are alive and being held, along with ten other Panamanian and Colombian hostages near Cristales.

They told us that the lads have been held, along with the other prisoners, as insurance against an attack. They have been used as forced farm labour but are being maintained in relatively good condition.

There is supposed to be a photo of the hostages and I am trying to get my hands on it.

What aggravates the situation is that the leader of the FARC 57th Front is in Panama under a false passport. The police hope to be able to get a dialogue going in the next couple of days.

To just grab him would most surely result in attacks on border villages and it would possibly hurt chances to negotiate for the hostages alive."

We are dubious about this rumour, as we were about the rumour a month ago that they were dead. We query everything now, after the Mike Hills affair and the rumours from Puerto Obaldia. The problem is that we hear everything third hand.

So I assured The Amercan that it would not raise false hopes.

It's likely that "a farm near Cristales" and "forced labour" are probably mis-translations, but that does not invalidate the possibility of other parts of it being true.

So I e-mailed FARC again: "Han usedes remitido a sus

direction nacional mi mensaje de Pablo Winder Y Tom Hart-
dyke que han desaparacido en Darien en Marzo.

Pablo is mi hijo primero. Lloro por el.

Eran mochileros, eran muy muy tontos.

Estamos conscientes de que hay rumores que estan se-
questados por la FARC en un granja cerca de Cristales.

Podriamos ayudar a que le FARC tuvieraun espacio en la
TV durante el momento de la liberatiuon dePablo y Tom.

Respeto su causa. Soy socio de Amnesty International, y
he pedido con frecuencia al Gobierno Colombiono clemencia para prisoneros.

Suplico os, suplico os contestar."

Translated: "There was sent to your national directorate
my message of Paul Winder and Tom Hart Dyke who had
disappeared in the Darien in March.

Paul is my eldest son. I weep for him.

They were backpackers. They were very very silly.

We are aware that there are rumours that they are held by
FARC in a farm near Cristales.

We could arrange that FARC could have a slot on TV at
the point at which Paul and Tom are freed.

We respect your cause. I am a member of Amnesty International, and I have frequently written to the Colombian
Government to have mercy on prisoners.

I beg you, I beg you to answer."

But no answer.

James Spring is, strange to say, more hopeful than ourselves. He wrote: "In this environment of misinformation, I
am afraid to hope. But I can't help it. I hope that your son is
alive and will be delivered to you soon.

But for my own sanity, I feel that I must restrict that hope so that my thinking remains clear enough to be of assistance should you need me."

And James Spring went on: "A lot of the story doesn't make sense. The American's statement about the lads being held to ensure that no attacks are effected against border FARC encampments presupposes that those who would be doing the attacking already know that the lads are there? Did the Panamanian Police know all the time about the lads' imprisonment by the FARC? Why would they not let you know? How could the police legally keep this info from the British embassies?"

Late in November

It had moved on towards the end of November and I had been waiting to see if this photograph turns up... but it is all rather mysterious. Why would an Indian walk around the jungle with a camera in his pocket? And The American spoke about a disk so it would be a digital camera. This dealing at third or fourth hand was very frustrating.

Nevertheless this news was very significant and I e-mailed FARC once again in late November, using roughly the same message as before, but saying that there was a rumour that the lads might be held near Cristales. If it was a dissident group that was holding them, then it would be no harm for FARC high command to know about it.

(For those interested in hind-sight, we found out later that the lads were released by the guerrillas about December 10th, ten to twelve days after this e-mail – perhaps the time needed for FARC to get the message into the jungle.)

31
INFORMATION FROM A PANAMANIAN CAPTIVE

December 1

We continued to wait and James Spring picked up information that made us realise that there is no foregone conclusion here.

James goes on to expand the picture: "The Associated Press wire yesterday reported a skirmish in the town of Frontino, not far from Cristales, where 15 people were killed.

Another little town in the same area, was the scene of a slaughter by FARC rebels who chased an escaped prisoner into the village and killed at least four people who would not reveal the escapee's whereabouts. I think that perhaps the Colombian army knows much more than they tell the Embassies.

I bet that they do all they can to suppress the info. By allowing the photos and info into the public domain, the Colombian government would be bolstering the cause of the rebels. The public would be afraid. The army would appear incompetent. Perhaps the Colombian government have admitted nothing because the information would draw the eyes of the world upon their ineptitude and their violations of human rights."

December 5

I am preparing to send out Christmas cards, and with

them some kind of cyclostyle summary of the situation, telling about the detectives that we had hired, about writing to FARC, about the rumour of them being dead, and the contrary rumour of a month later that they were alive and near the border at the Darien Gap, and then I added: "All is rumour and uncertain, and told at third or fourth hand; so we are always on tenterhooks."

That was all I could say, and I added that brief summary to the cards I have sent out today.

December 7

Events were still moving slowly in early December. I toyed with the idea of a radio advert offering a small reward of $500 or $1,000 for information. I suggested it to The American, but of course he poopooed it. Strange how all these people cannot see the difference between a reward for information and ransom money. When the chips are down they will not blink at $100,000 ransom money or $20,000 paid to one of the American negotiation agencies, but they balk at $500 for information, possibly paid to an Indian. The racialism is obvious.

12 December

Then, on December 12th,The American came out with some momentous news: "Yesterday, a 29 yr old Panamanian was released by the guerrillas after 14 months captivity. He told us that he was held in the Cristales area with several other people, including two young blonde foreigners. They were tall, thin and the one he talked to once in a while was called Tom. The other, he never spoke to.

The guerrilla group that is holding them is apparently a group loosely connected to the 57th Front. There are indications that there is some discontent in the ranks and many are serving under some duress but that hasn't been confirmed. The lads are apparently kept in the same camp but physically separated all the time.

The camp is moved frequently but stays in the area of Cristales, just across the border in Colombia from the Palo de las Leteras crossing. The one called Tom knew a few words of Spanish. According to this man, the lads are pretty thin and mosquito bitten but in fairly decent health. Later this afternoon our source was able to get a photo of the lads to the man and he identified the photos as the ones in the camp.

A ransom of between $30,000 and $49,000 was reportedly paid for the release of this Panamanian.

The father still has contact with the guerrillas and I just received a call indicating that he was willing to make contact on our behalf but would only deal with the parents and no one else. No police, press, church, no-one."

We expected to have to pay far more than $40,000 if a Panamanian had to pay that amount.

We started discussing with the Hart Dykes how we would deal with this, and we agreed at first that myself and Sarah Hart Dyke would offer to meet a guerrilla representative in a hut on the jungle edge to negotiate a ransom and a release. The intermediary would be the father of the Panamanian lad who had just been released.

That father agreed with that proposal provided only the

parents of the two boys were present, no officials or press, and then later he consented to a translator being present.

We suggested that James Spring be used as the translator because of his fluency in both Spanish and English, but The American was adamantly against him. I'm sure it was for the same reason as before – simple jealousy of an amateur with deeper knowledge than his, and antipathy because of James' deep respect for the culture of the native peoples.

The Hart Dykes were very keen that we use only official channels and "professional" negotiators. We believed that a low-key family and non-threatening approach as the Panamanian parent suggested would be far better.

The American was backing up the Hart Dykes, but uncertain whether he should recommend using someone from a US company, or the Colombian detective agency "who would deal with everything". They were suggesting firstly contacts with the FARC representative in Panama City done by his agent, and then a separate "Professional" Negotiator at $1250 a day stepping in – quite different from the low-key Panamanian father.

December 16

On December 16th The American came up with the proposed next step
"We have made an initial contact. I am told to expect a call sometime this week.
The group that is holding the lads is an organised FARC group, but something of a wild-card. Apparently they are 'moonlighting' in the kidnap business without the complete knowledge of the senior FARC leadership.

One or both of you should be making preparations to come to Panama in the relatively near future. If you use an advisor he must be a professional and be able to move in circles you thought only existed in the movies. The wrong move, comment, name in the papers, news article... and we are all in trouble.

I'll keep you posted on progress".

December 17

The Christmas cards that I sent out this weekend have a very different message attached. I tell briefly about the released Panamanian hostage, and our detective's efforts to get in contact with him as a contact point with the guerrillas... and that there seems to be now a strong likelihood that the lads are alive.

James Spring wrote: "It makes every nerve tingle. This sounds very, very good. The most promising, least questionable info so far. I am excited by the prospect of it all being true.

My questioning nature has been a good counter-weight for us often, so I won't turn it off yet.

We have hundreds of details to discuss... with the highest hopes ever."

However, Anne is just sending out Christmas cards with the simple "Happy Christmas" message, because she is taking seriously the warning about the danger of the story getting into the press and upping the ransom stakes.

So quite some confusion.

I am re-swatting my Spanish and thinking of arrangements to fly out to Panama for these talks.

The American is keeping his cards close to his chest. We don't know exactly what he is doing, and await more news.

32
JUNGLE CAPTIVES BACK FROM THE DEAD

On the evening of December 18th at about 10.30 pm there was a total surprise. We had a phone call from the British Embassy in Bogota, saying that Paul Winder and Tom Hart Dyke had been released by the guerrillas and that they had made their way to the village of Sautata. They had in fact been released 8 days ago! He also said that Paul had spoken to him on the radio from the park ranger's centre... And he had reported them as being both healthy.

What terrific news! I laughed and laughed, and Anne and I danced around the house.

What a relief!

The British Embassy said that they plan to get them to Turbo tomorrow, and then to Bogota.

We immediately phoned the American so that he would not waste further time on following the meeting-and-ransom plan. Interesting that he was trying to set up a meeting over the last week for captives who were no longer in captivity!

December 19

Early this morning I e-mailed James Spring and our relatives in Ireland and our close friends the news that we had been holding back for over a week: about the impending ransom talks, and then about the sudden release.

James Spring replied: "It has been a very emotional morning here in San Diego where all of my friends and family have been notified. My girlfriend can't stop crying about the beauty of it all."

We also phoned Sarah Hart Dyke immediately.

But Sarah Hart Dyke was very much against any newspapers being told about it until "long after" they are home – far more than what the British Embassy was asking which was until they are safe in Bogota. If I had my way I would have released the news immediately: once they were out of the jungle they were absolutely safe.

There was no need for silence. And anyway the British papers will find it out from the papers and the BBC in Bogota. We are one world.

Anne, out of kindness for the Hart Dyke's, and partly from a hangover through her believing The American line that Press coverage would increase ransom demands, is strenuously against anything leaking to the press.

I tried to discuss a rational attitude towards the press, but the Hart Dykes set impossible limits without any discussion. I realised that it was because of Anne's kind nature that she didn't want to disagree with Sarah Hart Dyke.

I went to my country dancing this evening, and let it out to a few people that good news would break soon – they had all known about the 9-month disappearance for a long time, and had been very sympathetic.

Then late evening we got a phone call from Paul. He's in Bogota at the British Embassy! That was fast. We thought it would take 2 days to get there

He told us the story of their planned escape and their storing up of food secretly, then of their release, and how they got lost in the swamps for 6 days, sometimes in water up to their chests, drinking from muddy pools, scavenging any wild fruit they thought would not kill them and meeting no-one and worrying that they would die of starvation; and how they went back to the guerrillas to get clearer directions… and how a junior FARC guerrilla said to them as they entered the camp, "Stay tonight. There is chicken tonight." But the guerrilla leader, after giving them clear instructions about how they had gone wrong, said, "If you come back we will shoot you." – for the obvious reason they might be leading the army back with them. Then, how they found their way out of the swamps to near the village of Sautata when a park ranger walked by… Then, how they could not believe the fuss that was made of them – they had been wondering how to make their $2 which the guerrillas left them stretch to get them across the Gulf of Uraba, and then they would have to hike a lift to Bogota – because they could not afford a bus.

Then, what happened instead: they were whisked off by a red-cross official in a speed-boat to Turbo, then by private jet to Apartado, and thence by major jet flight to Bogota all arranged for them.

So, Paul and Tom were collected in Bogota and received in the British Embassy. There they had a swimming-pool and a medical check-up and Ferrero Rocher chocolates.

What a contrast to the Third World they had been in.

It seemed the British Embassy might fly them home the next night.

December 19

But the press has got a hold of the story. It seems that the

Bogota journalists first heard of it, and the lads gave a press interview in Bogota.

Sarah Hart Dyke said, "When the press phoned me I just say 'No Comment' and put down the phone." When Anne went out shopping, she insisted that we don't contact the press because of Sarah's obsession against them. I agreed for peace sake.

But then the *Times* phoned up, and it seemed to me that they only wanted some perfectly reasonable details of the story, so I gave them basically what was my ever-changing Christmas card message, which told about the lead up to the ransom talks, about my e-mailing the guerrillas, and about the final release.

If the press basically know what has happened, and you don't speak to them, the press will just have to make up the detail themselves.

Of course, Anne was in a state when she heard I said anything to the press.

December 20

The story made headlines in all the papers.

The replies have been coming back from my brief message – ecstatic.

James Spring replied from San Diego with his usual eloquence: "My girlfriend is still an emotional mess. I have called all of my friends and family and they all send their most ecstatic congratulations. What a great Christmas!

I read the AP and *London Times* story. I'm curious about the negotiations that went on. Were there any truly?

And what happened to the guides that led the boys to Pay-ita – bad guys/good guys? I have a million questions. I'm so sorry to have expected the worst. I'm sorry that I couldn't go and collect info earlier.

The only saving thought in my head is that if such a unique set of circumstances allowed the boys to live, I'm glad that I didn't somehow upset that balance. It is a weak attempt at self-forgiveness, but the one to which I will cling until my full senses of reason return and the emotion begins to dissipate.

My whole life will change now. I will always remember that 99% is not 100%.

I have so many things that I want to say to you. But I think that they are all the same. Congratulations. I am happy for us all. I wish you very best in your opportunity to strengthen your relationship with your son. Your sons. Your wife. Everyone. Second chances like this are so rare.

We are all blessed. In the midst of my bliss-filled fog, I can see so much, so clearly now. Maybe the calendar critics were right. 2001 is the true start of a new millennium."

And our friends the Gillam's: "Happiness: I am so happy for you all. What a relief!"

"What can I say, life is beautiful."

In mid-afternoon the Television programme *Look-East* asked for an interview. Anne had gone to visit friends, and I racked my brain and phoned around to try to figure out where she had gone. I eventually found her, and drove around to fetch her to bring her to the local studios. She came reluctantly. She did the television, and I did the radio. She is more photogenic, and it all went down well.

In the evening the British Embassy in Bogota phoned to say that they would be on the plane tonight, arriving in Gatwick in the morning. The Foreign office phoned to say that the VIP lounge had been arranged to get us away from the crowds.

The Hart Dykes faxed us "Do not, I repeat, do not let anyone in the press know that they are flying home."

December 21

Anne says she hardly slept at all worried about what the press might make of it, and that she might offend Sarah Hart Dyke.

She takes all that The American says literally, how press coverage might be harmful to the remaining hostages, thinking that the mere mention of Cristales could have disastrous consequence.

The press were outside our house first thing in the morning. And the phone went all the time. We had to put it on answer-phone.

I had to go for my final cancer XRays in Colchester – I had been going for the last 5 weeks – and when I came back at lunchtime carrying the papers, the press were still at the house. I spoke to them and denied that we had any knowledge of when the lads were flying home.

It was obvious that the press knew. But I denied it because Anne and Sarah Hart Dyke imagine all kinds of things will proceed from speaking to the press.

The *Times* photographer most gently tried to persuade

Anne to let him take a few photographs, but Anne was still in her anti-newspaper mood. The photographer and the accompanying journalist stood in the freezing cold outside the door for nearly half an hour while I negotiated with Anne to let them in to take just a few photographs.

The newspaper reports contain far more information than we knew – either invented or got from Bogota – all quite harmless. Most of what I said to them doesn't seem to have got into the articles. No harm.

December 22

We left for Gatwick in late morning, wondering if the journalists would follow us; and we made and abandoned plans of using decoy cars. But they didn't follow us. They knew where we were going, and they knew that they had other reporters at the airport.

So much for thinking that we could keep the press off till the weeks ahead. In all, 17 newspapers or television or radio stations have contacted us, and because of the neuroticism about the press we haven't even phoned back most of them.

I've apologised to the Hart Dykes for giving the press a few crumbs of information.

The reunion at the airport involved great expectation, watching of television coverage, and in the final moment just joy. We get on very well with the Hart Dyke's, despite our very different attitude to the press. We let two photographers and a few journalists in to give a brief interview.

Paul said in a little speech at the airport: "The experience was a huge roller-coaster of emotions. There were low times, high times, terrifying times and fantastic times… our captors treated us well on the whole, and though they asked for $3.3 million ransom money each, they gave up when they had no way of communicating with the parents." Paul also described how they had befriended their captors and thus avoided confrontation. "The captors even went off to get anti-biotics when one of us developed an infection".

We drove back with Paul finding out more details of the 9 months, but that is his story.

December 22

We took our phone off the hook. The ecstatic messages still come in by e-mail.
People who had long ago contacted us and then drifted off when they realised that they could not help now swarmed back with congratulations.

A few examples.

"What fantastic news!
I just got a call from my brother. I've been trying to call but your phone is already constantly engaged! I'm utterly overwhelmed, as you all must be. When I spoke to my brother earlier, we were both just speechless, just sitting at either end of the phone mouthing unsayables and uttering occasional unconscious tiny yelps of joy, each of which in fact contain a booming cheer. I think we're now gonna have quite a celebration!"

"Words can't express the feelings I had upon hearing this news. I know that I don't really know you or your son but having been to the Darien and knowing all that you've been through the past months I felt a lot closer to the situation than most. I just wanted you to know that my thoughts were always with you and I'm so happy that this terrible saga has finally come to an end."

"I got a call from Steve at about 6 o'clock this evening and he told me this utterly fantastic news, I couldn't contain myself at first and I must have one got one or two strange looks on the Underground but who cares? I am so pleased that your long pursuit has paid such rich dividends as your courage and extreme resolve has been so apparent in the face of extreme adversity. Never has a happy ending been so richly deserved."

And from Fra Gabriel Guttierrez: "Siempre recordados amigos Brian y Ana Winder,
Con grande alegria recibi la noticia de la aparicion de Paul y Tom. Recibi la noticia por el Senor Lopes y despues mi familia telefono para mi para contarme que por la television y radio Colombiana se anuncio la liberacion de dos jovenes secuestrados de origen Ingles. Ofreci la Santa Misa para agradecer a Dios por el nacimiento de estos dos jovenes.
Ya puedo imaginar la grande alegria que sentis en vuestros corazones. Me une a esta grande alegria.
Mi familia en Colombia estan felices por este acontecimiento y les envian muchos recuerdos.
Fraternalmente."

Roughly translated: "My well-remembered friend,
I received news that Paul and Tom had reappeared.
I got this news both from Lopes Quichine, and also my family in Colombia who heard it on Radio and TV: they heard news of two English young men who had disappeared.

I offered a Mass of thanksgiving for their reappearance.

Can imagine the great joy you must feel in your hearts. I also am full of joy.

My family in Colombia is also delighted with the event and they send you their greetings.

With friendship.

Fra Gabriel."

And many other messages.

And the headings in the papers all said, "What a Christmas present."

And of course, the journalists got their wish – to report something cheerful for Christmas.

December 28

James Spring flew from San Diego in the USA to us in London and stayed a few days just after Christmas – such was his enthusiasm for the good news of Paul and Tom escaping from captivity. We together visited Lullingstone Castle where Tom lived and we celebrated together.

It had turned out well in the end.

33
RETROSPECT

A Retrospect

It is obvious that everyone involved learned a great deal during this long drawn-out affair and they were far wiser at the end than at the beginning.

The main thing I learned is that one cannot hurry things. Many things in life move slowly, and in difficult situations, it is often best to do nothing – just distract yourself with other activities and wait. Just endure it.

One problem was that the travellers' tales scared me excessively. People who were just passing through like Mike Pearson and Murray Vissor and even James Springs' initial narrative seemed to spread terror stories, but those with longer experience and in a stable situation like Jerry McDermott or the Herman, who ran the Bogota hostel, were balanced in their assessment that neither FARC nor the paramilitaries would harm foreigners.

But there were other things we learned as well.

When Paul and Tom came back and told their story it transpired that what the privately hired Indian Margarito Rosales, who could neither read nor write, had discovered was all valid – Paul and Tom had gone through the middle of the Darien Gap beyond Paya. What the official detective, The American, had "discovered" from his "reliable" sources – that they had gone North to Yape and then on to Puerto Obaldia and were dead – was all false.

Of course, The American did get valid information in the end because he was in a privileged position with the Panamanian police. That vital information was the naming of Cristales as their campt.

O course Mike Hills conned us badly. In retrospect, it amazed us that a person could himself endure deceiving for so long a period of time with ever-varying stories, especially when he got no second payment as a result. But all the way through we knew that he was a dodgy character, and we only used him because there seemed to be no-one else available. One clutches at straws in a shadowland of misinformation. But I was a fool for too long.

But it was very unlikely that any of this misinformation influenced what had got Paul and Tom released in the end nor did the detective agencies, in the end, solve the problem.
It is far more likely that the 5 emails to FARC did the trick, though we will never know for certain.
My last email to FARC identifying exactly the location where the group holding them were stationed was sent exactly a fortnight before they were released – just the length of time it might take for a message from FARC central command to a cut-off unit in the jungle. So we were beholden to the detective for the name of Cristales.
It is a reasonable hypothesis to say that the FARC group holding them was trying to make some money on the side by taking captives without the knowledge of Central Command.

If I had visited the eco-village, I might possibly have been able to contact the two guides, Albero and Eliseo, in Archya, and that might have satisfied my curiosity but it would not have got Paul and Tom released.

And finding the guides would not have been certain, because we do not know that they survived the ambush by FARC. We will never know.

We live and learn, even in our older years.

But it was also worth remembering that there are breakthrough points, without which the investigation could not have moved forward. In our story there were two vital ones:

The first breakthrough was opening up Paul's second email correspondence: from that there emerged such vital contacts as Patrician Upton, James Spring, the Hartdykes, Eric Nicolaison, and Margarito Rosales.

The second breakthrough was finding an email address for FARC.

34
AFTERMATH

The immediate aftermath of the return home was that Paul and Tom wrote a book together on their adventure called *The Cloud Garden*. It was on the best-seller list for a while. The name was derived from the characteristics of the high-altitude forest where they mainly moved around during their capture and which was an ideal environment for the orchids that Tom was fascinated by.

After he came back, Tom went on to build a World Garden in the grounds of his family home, Lullingstone Castle in Kent. That itself was an adventure and he wrote a book on it called *An Englishman's Home*. What was significant was that in order to get the funding for that, the family courted publicity as much as they could, whereas they had been highly against publicity during the 9 months search. Tom also appeared on many TV programmes – especially on the subject of Orchids.

And the two families, the Winders and the Hart Dykes, are still very good friends.

Paul took to other forms of adventure – climbing mountains. Every year he still spends part of the summer months in the Alps or Yosemite Valley or other places. In this he follows the footsteps of his uncle Frank who was a co-founder of the Irish Mountaineering club in the 1940s.

A very good program followed some time later on the

BBC comparing 4 incidents of young people who disappeared abroad, one hang-gliding in Northern India, one joining a Hari-Krishna sect in Dublin, one beach-combing in Mexico, and Tom and Paul. Tom and Paul were the only ones who came home at the time of the film's making. It is still a fascinating CD.

Sadly Lucie Blackman was found to have been murdered by a Japanese businessman and buried in a cave long before Mike Hills defrauded her parents on the subject.

As for Mike Hills, here is what happened.

The British police failed to arrest Mike Hills for 2 years. The fraud involved was probably below the limit for getting him extradited from Holland. Then they got information from Interpol that he had moved to Spain.

The police did not keep us informed during all this period.

In December 2002 Mike Hills returned to Britain because his common law wife needed treatment for cancer. He was not picked up at the ports, but he made a mess of parking a car in London and the police were called in. The policeman dealing with it tapped his name into his hand-held computer, and discovered that Mike Hills was wanted for other reasons. He was arrested.

At Chelmsford court on April 23rd of 2003, he admitted guilt in defrauding the Blackman's and the Winder's by accepting money on the pretence of searching for the missing people, Lucie Blackman and Paul Winder. Since he pleaded guilty, we were given no opportunity to expose all the lies he told over many months.

Despite that admission in court, he still could not get out of his habit of lying, and he said to reporters after the trial

that he had handed the Blackman's money over to his underworld contacts in Japan, whereas in fact he had no such.
Leopards do not change their spots.

Finally, in June 2003 Mike Hills was sentenced to three
and a half years imprisonment.

THE END

BIOGRAPHY

Brian Winder is a family man with three grown-up sons and a long-suffering wife who is a French teacher. He was born and educated with degrees in Classics and Philosophy with the Jesuits in Ireland. In his 20s, he travelled in North Africa and most countries in Europe, and most interestingly in Russia when it opened its borders. He taught and worked in Zambia for 11 years and in London, after he specialised in computers and as an accountant. After retirement, he devoted himself entirely to volunteering with many roles in charities serving the homeless and addicts for over 25 years. His favourite hobby was country dancing.